contents

Introduction

When you work in the building trade, it is not uncommon to be approached by family or friends, or indeed friends of friends, or in fact anybody who can get hold of you, and asked the odd bit of advice on DIY. In fact when you work in the building trade, you might as well put a large sticker on your back with *DIY helpline* and your telephone number next to it. When the call comes at 11.30 p.m., it can be a little annoying, but in general those phone calls do give you a feeling of being wanted, and indeed most of us in the business like nothing more than passing the time of day, imparting our tried and tested tips and advice onto less experienced DIYers. In fact, in that moment where you solve someone's lifelong quest to fix some shelves in a level position, or

ask

the 1000 most asked questions about
the home

Julian Cassell &
Peter Parham

spruce

A Hachette Livre UK Company

First published in Great Britain in 2009 by Spruce,
a division of Octopus Publishing Group Ltd.
2–4 Heron Quays, London E14 4JP
www.octopusbooks.co.uk
www.octopusbooksusa.com

Copyright © Octopus Publishing Group Ltd 2009
Text copyright © Julian Cassell and Peter Parham 2009

Illustrated by Tim Wesson

Distributed in the United States and Canada
by Hachette Book Group USA
237 Park Avenue
New York NY 10017

ISBN 13 978-1-84601-292-1
ISBN 10 1-84601-292-9

CIP catalogue record of this book is available from the British Library.

Printed and bound in China

10 9 8 7 6 5 4 3 2 1

provide someone with the right instruction on how to fix a bathroom slow drip without unleashing a tidal wave through the house; yes, in that moment of gratitude, when that person has previously been breaking, bodging or feeling generally inadequate, yes in that moment, you do feel that you could have saved a marriage, saved an injury, or at the very least, saved someone from more years of frustration and generally devaluing their home.

Therefore, in this book, we have tried to cover the most commonly asked questions that we have experienced during our years in the trade. We've tried to keep things sharp and to the point, as the other thing you soon realize when imparting the aforementioned advice, is that as soon as you start to go into too much detail, or go off at too much of a tangent: firstly the eyes of the person asking the question begin to glaze over, and secondly, they begin to fear the task more than when they initially sought help.

What we have also tried to do is cover as many levels of DIY as possible in terms of aptitude. With the questions we get asked, it becomes more and more apparent that some people literally don't know which end of a drill to hold, whilst others will seek advice on the best metal or alloy used to make a specific drill bit. Therefore we hope we have provided questions and answers for all levels of ability and interest. We also hope that even the most experienced DIYer will find some ideas that they have not tried or heard of before. After all we keep learning every day and finding better ways to tackle some jobs, and so the next 1000 answers are already beginning to develop.

Therefore in this book, we hope that you will find answers to some of your most longstanding DIY questions and hopefully we may pre-empt some future ones. DIY can be the most infuriating of pastimes when things aren't going to plan, but when it all comes good, it is a very satisfying place to be. We wish you good luck with your work.

Maintenance

& repair

"My smoke alarm keeps beeping from time to time. Is it broken?"

No, it means the battery needs replacing. DO IT NOW.

"Do smoke alarms need servicing?"

Regularly check that the batteries are working (even on mains-operated models as they still have a battery back-up). Also check the casing to see when the manufacturer recommends replacement.

"How many smoke alarms do I need?"

A minimum of one on each floor, probably in the hall and on the landing.

"How often does my boiler need servicing?"

Most boilers should be serviced once a year.

"I've got so much stuff that needs servicing, how do I keep on top of things?"

Keep a house journal with times and schedules so that you know when something needs to be serviced.

"There are sooty deposits above my gas fire. Is this a problem?"

Yes, get it inspected immediately.

"I have a real fire. How often should the chimney be swept?"

At least once a year.

"If something electrical looks slightly burnt, is it still safe?"

NO. Stop using it and get it checked by a qualified electrician.

"When I removed a lampshade, I cracked the part of the bulb holder that holds the shade. Do I need to replace the lot?"

No, you can buy a new bulb holder and simply use the threaded ring as a straight replacement. It means you won't have to do any wiring.

"My dimmer switch makes a humming noise. Is this safe?"

Yes, most of them do.

"How do I know which fuse is which in my fuse box?"

They should have labels (often inside the cover). If not, do it yourself: turn all lights and appliances on and see what cuts out when you remove a fuse or, on a modern consumer unit, when you turn off a miniature circuit breaker.

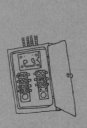

"My fuse box looks very old. Should I change it?"

Ideally yes; get an electrician to advise you. A modern consumer unit is much easier to operate and has more safety features, such as cutting the power when there is a problem.

"My lamp fuse keeps blowing. Can I put a bigger one in?"

No, there is clearly a fault with the lamp. Have it checked by an electrician before using it again.

"Our new home has a very modern electric box, and every time a bulb blows, all the lights go off. Is this normal?"

Modern consumer units are very sensitive, and this is perfectly normal. It is for your own protection.

"I have a loose electrical socket. How do I tighten it up?"

Make sure the power is turned off at the consumer unit or fuse box. Loosen the face plate. Pull the plate to one side and re-fix the back box, drilling new holes and inserting fresh wall plugs if required before screwing in place.

"My electrical sockets aren't level. How can I adjust them?"

Make sure the power is turned off at the consumer unit or fuse box. Loosen the screws holding the face plate in position. You'll find there will be a bit of play to allow you to adjust the position of the box behind.

"My toaster won't work. How do I know if it's broken?"

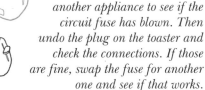

First check the socket using another appliance to see if the circuit fuse has blown. Then undo the plug on the toaster and check the connections. If those are fine, swap the fuse for another one and see if that works.

"My ceiling light won't work. Why?"

Try replacing the bulb. If that doesn't work check the circuit fuse has not blown. If that doesn't work, turn the power off at the fuse box or consumer unit and check the connections in the bulb holder.

"The pull cord switch for my bathroom light has broken. Can it be fixed?"

No, the whole unit needs replacing.

"My electric oven is fine but the spark ignition for my gas rings doesn't work anymore. Surely this can't be an electrical fault?"

If the ignition switch is not faulty, it may well have fused. Your oven still works because hobs and ovens are often fused separately.

"The flex on my lamp is looking a bit frayed. Is this ok?"

Use electrical insulation tape as a temporary repair, but replace the flex as soon as you can.

"Can I glue a cracked electrical socket back together?"

No. Replace it.

"We've moved to a new house with sunken low-voltage lights. How do I change a bulb?"

There are three possible ways. First is using a round wire clip, which presses together to allow the bulb to drop down. Second is by unscrewing the threaded inner edge of the fitting. Third, common on low-energy lights, is to attach a special sucker to the bulb and twist to remove it.

"Can we change low-voltage lights for low-energy ones?"

In most cases yes, but get a qualified electrician to advise you.

"Can I use low-energy bulbs on dimmers?"

No, not yet, but manufacturers are working on it.

"How do I remove a smashed light bulb?"

Make sure the power is turned off at the consumer unit or fuse box. Use pliers to grab the metal part of the bulb (the part that goes in the fitting) and turn to ease it free.

"The heavy ceiling light in my bedroom has pulled away from the ceiling. How can I support it?"

Go up to the loft and screw a block of wood between the joists where you want the light positioned. This will give you a secure fixing area.

"My extractor fan doesn't stay on for very long. Why?"

There is usually a timer on the motor, so adjust it to come on for longer if you like.

"My extractor fan seems to vent straight into my loft space. Is this ok?"

No, it should be directed through an outside wall or through the roof, otherwise you're filling the loft with moist air.

"My extractor fan is very quiet. How do I know if it's working?"

Some modern ones are very quiet. Hold a sheet of tissue paper against it: if it stays there, it means the extractor is working.

"My shower cubicle ceiling is showing signs of poor ventilation: flaky paint and nasty black patches?"

Fix a thin sheet of UPVC to the ceiling using grab adhesive, and seal the edges with silicone.

"My corner shower is leaking through the silicone seal around the tray, which I've only just redone. Why can this be?"

It's probably leaking at the base of the enclosure wall channels. Unscrew the enclosure, seal along the joints on the outside of the channel with silicone and refit the enclosure.

"My shower just dribbles. How can I improve it?"

You can fit a pump if you have a tank-fed water system.

"Why has the flow from my shower reduced so much?"

As long as there is no problem with your water system, it could simply be that the head is coated with limescale. Take it apart and soak in de-scaling solution before reassembly.

"The seal on my shower keeps peeling away. Why?"

Probably because the cleaner you are using (limescale removers especially) is allowed to sit on the seal for too long. Rinse more quickly in future, or change your brand of cleaner.

"I live in a hard water area and my bathroom fittings become coated in limescale. How can I get rid of it?"

The best permanent solution is to fit a water softener.

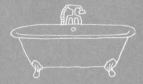

"The seal around the edge of my bath is flaking and I think it may be leaking. How do I repair it?"

Scrape the old silicone off using a window scraper, or a special silicone remover. Clean the edge really thoroughly before applying a new bead of silicone.

"How do I apply silicone sealant neatly?"

Run two strips of masking tape either side of the joint. Apply the sealant with a constant flow along the joint. Smooth with a dampened finger, remove the tape and smooth again.

"In my bathroom, the wallpaper keeps lifting at the bottom. How can I cure this?"

Stick it back down with PVA or border adhesive, allow it to dry thoroughly, then apply a thin bead of clear silicone sealant along the top of the skirting board where it meets the paper edge.

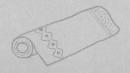

"My plastic bath seems to move when I get in it. How can I strengthen it?"

Take off the panel and add extra wooden supports to the underside.

"I've got a chip in my enamel bath. Can it be repaired?"

Yes, there are lots of different repair kits on the market for just such accidents.

"Can marks on a bath be removed?"

In some cases yes. Manufacturers produce bath rubbers that can be used to help remove stubborn marks on both enamel and plastic baths.

"What is the switch above my bathroom door?"

Most likely the fan isolator switch. If you turn it off, your bathroom extractor fan will stop working.

"How do I stop water leaking from the top of my radiator?"

It's probably coming out of the bleed valve. Get a radiator bleed key and tighten up the valve.

"Water is dripping out of the valve bit where it joins the bottom of my radiator. What shall I do?"

You'll need two adjustable spanners or wrenches. Hold the main body of the tap (valve) while you tighten the nut below it or to the side of it. BE GENTLE, or you risk fracturing the joint and making things worse.

"My radiator is not as warm as it used to be, and it's hot at the bottom and cold at the top. What can I do?"

You've got an air lock. Use a bleed key at the top corner of the radiator. Don't take the tiny nut out, just loosen it until you hear hissing (the air coming out). Hold a cloth next to it and as soon as water appears, tighten it back up.

"How can I get the most heat out of my radiators?"

Use reflective foil on the
walls behind them to direct
maximum heat into the room.

"How can I make my heating system more efficient?"

*Make sure that all your radiators are fitted
with thermostatic radiator valves (TRVs).*

"I've bled my radiators, but my heating doesn't work at all now. What's wrong?"

You must have a combi-boiler or pressurized system. You'll need to briefly open the valve on the filling loop by the boiler to re-pressurize the system. Refer to your boiler instruction manual.

"My toilet cistern makes a terrible noise when I flush it. Is there a problem?"

Nine times out of ten, the float valve washer needs replacing.

"My toilet cistern is filling constantly. What can I do as it's wasting so much water?"

You need to adjust the float valve arm so the water intake stops when the cistern is full. Plastic ones tend to have a screw adjustment; metal ones can be bent.

"How do I unblock my toilet – plungers and chemicals don't seem to work?"

Buy a hand-held auger that will 'burrow' down into the pipes and help move a blockage.

"Why doesn't my toilet flush first time when the cistern seems to be full?"

It sounds like the outlet valve is not working properly and should be replaced. This could be one of many types, but all are easy to replace.

"I have an old toilet, and someone told me to put a brick in my cistern to save water. Is this okay?"

Adding the brick will take up volume and therefore reduces the amount of water in the cistern. Wrap it in plastic first to avoid the brick degrading and possibly blocking the valves.

"What is a valve?"

It's another word for a tap (faucet).
Generally 'valves' are in the middle of a
pipe run, while 'taps' are at the end.

"Whenever I turn on the kitchen tap (faucet), there's an awful banging noise. How can I stop it?"

This is water hammer and is due to pipes not being fixed to the wall. Try turning down the main stop cock half a turn and adding a few pipe clips, especially on long runs of pipe.

"Why won't my plunger unblock the bathroom basin?"

Probably because you haven't built up suction pressure by covering the overflow at the same time. Hold a damp cloth over it as you move the plunger up and down.

"The washers on my taps (faucets) keep having to be replaced. Why?"

Because you are tightening the tap too much when you turn it off. Be gentle: a tap will always drip a little after it has been turned off.

"My kitchen tap is leaking at the base of the spout. Surely this isn't the washer?"

No, it's an O-ring seal, which is common on spouts that swivel. There'll be a tiny grub screw or similar at the base of the spout. Unscrew it, pop the spout off, replace the O-ring and reassemble.

"How do I find my mains stopcock?"

It is likely to be close to the kitchen sink at ground level, or sometimes by the downstairs toilet. Make sure you locate it: it's important!

"Do I always have to turn the stopcock off when working on fittings in my home?"

No, some fittings have isolation valves on the pipes next to the fitting. Always check here first.

"My stopcock is jammed. How can I loosen it off?"

Try easing it with some lubricating oil. When you get it to move, open it fully again, then turn it back a quarter turn or so to prevent it seizing in the future.

"Why do my compression joints leak?"

Try winding some PTFE tape around the thread before you tighten them up.

"Can I use plastic pipe to repair a section in a copper water pipe?"

Yes, but check that the pipe can deal with hot water. Bear in mind that most plastic pipe cannot be used close to a boiler.

"My basin waste pipe is dripping. What's the solution?"

Dismantle it and replace any rubber seals and washers.

"Why is water running out of my basin so slowly?"

You've probably got a blockage. First unscrew the bottle trap below and check it is clear. If so, try pushing a piece of stout wire (such as an straightened coat hanger) into the pipe and pulling back any debris. It's normally hair!

"What's the first thing to do if I need to change a tap (faucet) washer?"

Make sure the water is turned off at the stopcock or an isolation valve. If you have an old water system, you may need to drain your hot or cold water tanks or cylinders too.

"How do I take a tap (faucet) apart?"

There is often a tiny grub screw on the head. This may be hidden below the little caps that label the hot and cold.

"Why do washers on cold water taps (faucets) need replacing most often?"

It's due to the mains pressure.

"Can I adjust the water mains pressure into my house?"

No, but you can turn your stopcock up or down to adjust the water pressure inside your home.

"I've taken my tap (faucet) apart to replace the washer, but I can't find one to replace. Where's it gone?"

You've probably got taps/faucets that use ceramic disc cartridges. Replace the whole cartridge.

"I want to replace my kitchen tap but I can't reach underneath the sink to loosen it off. What do I do?"

You'll need a basin spanner, which has a long handle to allow you to reach into awkward areas.

"I've got plastic push-fit waste pipes, but they won't push together! What's going on?"

They can be tight, so try lubricating the end of the pipe with some washing-up liquid.

"What do I do if I have a leaking water pipe?"

If you can, turn off the water supply to that part of the pipe at the appropriate isolating valve. If this isn't possible, turn off at the mains stopcock. If it's a heating pipe, also turn the heating off.

"What's the best way to replace a short section of copper pipe?"

There are many ways, but one is to use a slip coupling. Another is to use a push-fit hose.

"Should I replace lead pipes?"

If they are supply pipes, then you definitely should. Waste pipes should also be replaced, although they aren't such a problem because you don't drink the water that runs through them.

"Can old pipes and taps (faucets) be recycled?"

Yes, all of them.

"My doors rattle with the slightest breeze and it's driving me mad. How can I stop them?"

You will have to move the door stop (the thin strip of wood that the door closes on to), or the strike plate (the bit on the frame that the latch closes into).

"My door has bowed. Is there anything I can do to help it close?"

It's almost impossible to straighten a door. Therefore, remove the door stop, close the door, and refit the doorstop to account for the awkward profile. Once painted in, no one will notice.

"My door sticks. Is there a simple way to ease it?"

You need to plane a little wood off the edge of the door, which will be easier if you take it off its hinges. An ideal gap around the door is 2–3 mm ($\frac{1}{16}$–$\frac{1}{8}$ in).

"When I try to plane the edge of my door, it keeps snagging the wood. What's wrong?"

The blade is blunt and needs sharpening, or the mouth of the plane is set too proud. Adjust the blade position.

"I'm trying to unscrew the hinges on my door, but they've been painted over. How do I loosen them?"

Use a craft knife to scrape grooves in the screw heads. Then use the right size screwdriver, initially giving it a tap with a hammer to break the paint seal.

"The screws holding my door hinges on are wobbly. How can I strengthen them?"

Remove the screws and try tapping some matchsticks into the holes to make them smaller before putting the screws back in.

"I've changed my door around to hang on the opposite side of the frame. How do I repair the old hinge holes?"

Cut blocks of wood to fit, making them slightly deeper than the holes. Glue them in place, let them dry, then plane them flush with the door frame.

"The retaining screws on my door knob keep loosening. Can I tighten them up?"

Try removing the handle and rotating the fixing plate. Drill pilot holes in the new positions and refit the handle.

"How do I ease a sticking lock?"

Use an aerosol penetrating oil with a filament attachment that lets you get right inside the keyhole.

"Why doesn't my door latch catch properly when I close the door?"

The strike plate is probably badly positioned. Before you move it, try filing the inner edge of the plate to enlarge the hole.

"I've broken a pane of glass in my dining room door. Can I use any glass to replace it?"

No, it must be toughened safety glass.

"I've got an old door with a big gap at the top. I don't want to replace it, so can I fix it?"

Yes, simply cut a section of batten to fit and glue and screw it along the top edge of the door.

"My door seems to bind on the hinges, making it difficult to close. What can I do?"

Remove the hinges and pack stiff card behind them before refitting.

"My door catches on the sloping kitchen floor as it opens. If I plane it down too much, I'll end up with a big gap under it when it's closed. What should I do?"

Try fitting rising butt hinges as these lift the door as it opens.

"How can I stop my doors slamming?"

Fit door closers on the top edges of the doors.

"How do I seal my door against the winter cold?"

Screw a brush seal along the bottom edge.

"Can I still open my electric garage door in a power cut?"

Yes, as all models have a manual override system, where you can use it like a normal garage door.

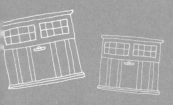

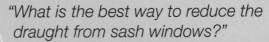

"What is the best way to reduce the draught from sash windows?"

You can buy and fit brush draught excluders, but you'll probably have to take out the sashes and refit them properly if you want to avoid all draughts.

"The handle on my UPVC window has snapped. Can it be replaced?"

Yes. If you look closely, it should be possible to flick off the fixing covers with a flat-head screwdriver. Then simply unscrew and replace.

"My UPVC French doors don't seem to shut properly. How can I close them if I can't plane them down?"

Most UPVC door hinges have a socket in which you insert an Allen key to adjust the door position.

"How can I stop the draught around the front door?"

Pin a draught excluder to the outside frame.

"Why are some of my double-glazed windows always misty?"

The seal on the unit is broken. Check your guarantee, because the unit will need replacing.

"The wind whistles through my windows. What should I do?"

Simply use self-adhesive foam strips around all edges of the window. It's easily cut to fit with a craft knife.

"There's a messy gap around the edge of my UPVC windows. How can I smarten them up?"

Buy some strips of upvc (cover strips) and use silicone to fix them over the gap to give a neater finish.

"My windows have just been painted and now I can't open them. How can I ease them?"

Run a sharp craft knife around the join between the window and the frame. This should loosen things up.

"How do I know where pipes and cables are if I'm trying to repair a floor?"

A pipe and cable detector will help.

"The wind is whistling through my letterbox. What can I do?"

Simple; just screw a letterbox brush draught excluder on the inside.

"Is it really true that keyholes can cause heat loss from your home?"

You'd be amazed how much. Simply screw on a special moveable cover plate.

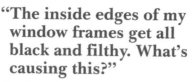

"The inside edges of my window frames get all black and filthy. What's causing this?"

Condensation, so try improving ventilation in the room. Open windows more often.

"How can I stop my windows rattling in the wind?"

Adjust the catch to ensure it closes tighter, or try repositioning the mortise plate (the metal plate on the window frame into which the catch fits).

"Can a tongue and groove panel with a split be repaired?"

Yes, cut down through the tongue of the split board using a pad saw (you might need to drill a hole first to get the point of the saw in). Lever out the board. Cut a new one to length, remove its tongue with a chisel and pin the board in place.

"When I'm doing repairs, how do I stop my safety goggles steaming up?"

Consider buying wrapround safety specs instead as there is better air flow around the edges.

"How do I take really accurate measurements?"

Try using a digital tape measure.

"I'm replacing my hacksaw blade. Which way round does it go?"

The teeth must be pointing forwards.

"Can I get an old saw blade sharpened?"

It is difficult to find someone who can do it now. Instead, keep the old saw for rough jobs, like cutting insulation boards and plasterboard.

"How do I sharpen a chisel?"

You need a sharpening stone. Hone the angled side first and then the flat side to provide a sharp, burr-free edge. Some stones need water, others oil. You can buy a special honing guide to hold the chisel at the right angle.

"How do I sharpen a plane?"

Take the blade out and sharpen it just like a chisel.

"I've got lots of home repairs to do. Do I need lots of expensive tools?"

No, start with the basics: hammer, screwdrivers, handsaw, tape measure, adjustable spanner, craft knife, chisels and a spirit level. It's also good to have a cordless drill/screwdriver.

"What basic safety equipment do I need when carrying out home repairs?"

Goggles or safety specs, work gloves, dust mask, ear plugs/defenders and sturdy shoes.

"My dust mask doesn't protect me from paint fumes. Why?"

Because it's designed just to stop dust. You need a special respirator mask.

"The first few turns of driving a screw into wood are very difficult. Is there a trick?"

Use a carpenter's bradawl. This is basically a metal point on a handle that you can push into the wood to make a starting hole for the screw.

"What's the best way to stop floorboards squeaking?"

Screw them down rather than nail them. Drill pilot holes and take care not to go through any pipes or cables!

"My floorboard replacements are shallower than the existing ones. What can I use to level them?"

Use strips of hardboard on the joists to raise the board level.

"My floorboard replacements are deeper than the existing ones. How can I adjust them?"

Mark the positions of the joists on the boards and chisel out some channels in the boards.

"How do I lift a tongue and groove floorboard?"

First you need to cut down the gap on either side of the board with a floorboard saw or circular saw to cut off the tongues. Take care not to cut through pipes or cables. The board may then be levered up.

"How do I stop knots coming out of my wooden floor?"

You can't really stop them, but you can use wood adhesive to glue them back in. Loosen the knot, fill the hole with plastic wood and sand it smooth.

"How do I fit a new tongue and groove board when repairing the floor?"

Chisel off the tongue of the new board before you fix it in place.

"My floorboards are very old and I need to replace one. How can I find an old board to match?"

With difficulty. It's better to take another up from an inconspicuous area (under the sofa, for example) and use this as a replacement. Then use a new board under the sofa where it won't be seen.

"How can I fill the gaps between my floorboards?"

Use thin strips of wood glued and wedged in place. Allow the glue to dry, then plane smooth.

"I need to replace a floorboard at the base of my door frame, but it is an awkward shape. Any ideas?"

Use the old broken one as a template or get a profile gauge that gives you a guideline for tricky profiles.

"My carpet was wet and when I rolled it back, the concrete floor below was damp. What could cause this?"

It's not good news: it could be a leaking pipe or rising damp. Get the professionals to check.

"I've just dropped a saucepan on my tiled floor and cracked a tile. How can I repair or replace it?"

Drill lots of small holes in the tile to help break it up so that it may be removed easily, along with the old adhesive. Pop a new tile in its place.

"My bedroom floor has a big dip in it. Is this something to worry about?"

It could be nothing, so don't panic. However, the joists could be failing so get an expert to investigate further.

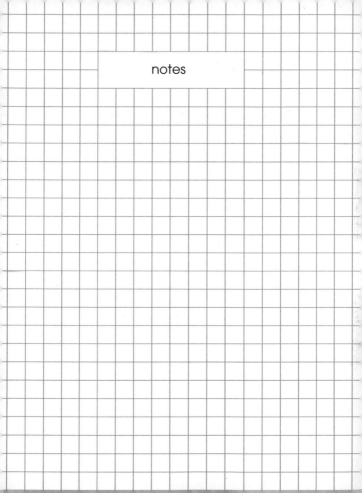

notes

"How do I avoid damaging surrounding floorboards when I prise an old one out?"

Rest the edge of your pry bar on a block of wood.

"I need to replace a section of old skirting board, but can't find the right style. Where should I look?"

It can be very difficult. It would be easier to buy a softwood plank and use a router with the correct bit(s) to make your own. If you aren't confident with a router, pay a joiner to do it for you.

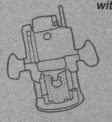

"I've got some paint splatters on my carpet. How can I remove them?"

Let it dry thoroughly: don't try wiping it when wet. Use a craft knife to gently tease the dry paint from the carpet piles by brushing the surface of the blade across the top surface of the paint spot.

"How do I repair a chip in my laminate floor?"

Buy a scratch repair kit. Mix the compound, press it in the hole and scrape off the excess.

"My dog scratches the paintwork at the bottom of our back door when he asks to go out. Any ideas?"

Fix a strip of aluminium over the affected area.

"Can I repair a scorch mark in my vinyl floor?"

Yes. Make a square panel repair. Position a new piece of flooring over the damaged area. Cut down through both pieces with a craft knife. Remove the old section and glue the new piece in place.

"I've got a stain in my carpet that won't clean. What are my options?"

Position a round shape, such as a saucepan lid, over the stain. Cut round it with a craft knife and remove the damaged section. Cut out a similar shape on a replacement piece and stick it in the hole, using a spray adhesive to keep it in place.

"How do I stop stairs squeaking?"

Ideally, you need to get underneath them. Fit wooden wedges in any joints, and screw triangular wood blocks into the corners where the risers meet the treads.

"My stairs creak and I can't get underneath them. Help!"

Drill a hole and spray in some expanding foam to support the stairs (as long as the void underneath isn't too big!).

"How do I repair a big hole in my plasterboard wall?"

Use a pad saw to cut the hole to a square, so that the vertical edges of the square lie over the upright studs (timber) in the walls. Cut and fit two more studs to lie behind the horizontal edges of the square. Cut a new piece of plasterboard to fit and screw it to the studs with drywall screws. The joints can then be taped and the patch plastered.

"The wall keeps cracking around the flue from my wood burner. How can I stop this?"

Instead of using mortar or plaster, use fire cement to fill any cracks.

"A small patch of plaster has come away from my wall. How should I fill it?"

Prime the area with PVA solution (1 part PVA to 4 parts water). Press in some interior filler, let it dry then sand it smooth.

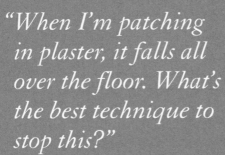

"When I'm patching in plaster, it falls all over the floor. What's the best technique to stop this?"

Hold a hawk (a small platform with handle underneath) to catch any plaster as it falls.

"I have a hole in the middle of my plasterboard wall that is too big to fill. What should I do?"

Cut a length of batten slightly longer than the hole is wide. Insert it through the hole with the ends against the back of the plasterboard on each side. Screw through the plasterboard into both ends to hold the batten in place. Cut a piece of plasterboard to fit the hole and screw into the batten.

"Do I need to use lime plaster when patching old lath and plaster walls?"

No, you can use normal plaster to good effect.

"Where can I find replacement sections for my old plaster cornice?"

Look on the internet, where you can find nearly every design now. If not, you can commission it direct from a manufacturer.

"A section of coving has come away from my wall. How should I repair it?"

Prise it back enough to squeeze some grab adhesive behind it. Press it back in place and use two nails in the wall as temporary support while it dries.

"What's the best way of mixing small quantities of plaster?"

In a bucket with a mixing paddle attachment for your electric drill.

"Bits of tape seem to be coming away from my wall surface. What is happening?"

Your walls are dry lined and the scrim tape used between boards has lifted. Cut the loose section of tape out, put a new section in its place and fill over the top.

"The base of my living room wall is damp. Is this serious?"

First check there is no soil piled up on the out side. If not, you may have rising damp. Call in a professional, as the walls may need injecting with chemicals and you may need some waterproof rendering.

"There's a small damp patch on my wall. Can you help?"

Check the brick work outside to see if there is a gap in the pointing. The damp patch may alternatively be caused by a blocked gutter or down pipe.

"What is rising damp?"

Rising damp is the movement of moisture up through walls and floors where there is no waterproof membrane. Rising damp will only reach 1.2 m (4 ft) above ground level.

"I'm replacing skirting boards but the backs of the old ones are covered with white strands and there's an awful musty smell. Should I be worried?"

It sounds like dry rot, so get a professional to advise you.

"How do I know if the woodworm in my beams is active?"

Check directly below the holes for little piles of dust.

"Can I treat woodworm myself?"

Yes, for localized areas. For larger areas, get in a professional firm.

"I've got mice in my loft. What should I do?"

First try using bait and traps. If this doesn't work, get the environmental health officer in.

"How can I stop the wind coming down an old chimney?"

Fit a chimney balloon. These inflate at the bottom to create a seal.

"Why are there damp patches on my chimney breast?"

It's damp seeping through from inside the chimney. If the chimney has been capped, you may need some ventilation: knock out a brick in the chimney breast and fit a vent.

"My kitchen cupboard doors don't line up any more. What's happened?"

Don't worry, doors and hinges can move slightly with time. Most hinges on kitchen cupboards are adjustable. Use a screwdriver at the appropriate point on the hinge to level up.

"How can I stop my kitchen drawers banging closed?"

Fit soft-close runners on the drawers. A cheaper and quicker option is self-adhesive pads to reduce the noise.

"Can I repair a chipped laminate worktop?"

Yes, if you've still got the piece that has come off. Use contact adhesive to stick it back down, holding it in place with masking tape while it dries.

"I have a loose kitchen drawer handle. What can I do?"

You'll need to strengthen the fixing by fitting a washer next to the screw head and putting some contact adhesive on the thread of the handle as you tighten it.

"How can I make my bespoke kitchen drawers run more smoothly?"

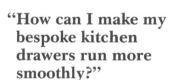

Rub some candle wax on the wooden runners.

"Can I adjust metal drawer runners if the drawers are not level?"

Yes. Most runners have lots of predrilled holes precisely for this purpose.

"The joints in my wooden worktop have opened up. How can I fill them?"

Buy several different plastic wood fillers and blend them to match your worktop. Press in place and sand smooth before oiling.

"I've got awful ring marks on my wooden kitchen worktop where people keep leaving their coffee cups. How can I get rid of them?"

Use a power sander: a palm sander is ideal. This will remove the marks and then you can simply reseal the worktop.

"My kitchen cupboard door hinge has pulled out of its chipboard surround. Can I fix this?"

Yes, simply move the hinge plate and hinge further down the door and frame. You'll need a hinge-cutting bit to drill a new hole for the hinge on the door.

"My fitted kitchen sink wobbles all over the place. What can I do?"

Check underneath and tighten the retaining clips that hold it in place.

"My kitchen wall units aren't level. Is there any way of moving them?"

Yes, you'll normally find adjusting blocks inside the cupboards in the top corners. Rotate the screws accordingly to adjust the level.

"One of my kitchen units is wobbly. How can I fix it?"

Take off the plinth and you may find that the adjustable legs need unscrewing slightly.

"The plinth below my kitchen units keeps coming off. How can I strengthen it?"

Add extra clips or, at the top of the plinth (so it won't be seen), put a few screws directly through the plinth into the unit legs.

"How do I keep my steel extractor fan hood clean?"

Put a tiny dab of baby oil or olive oil on a kitchen towel and polish the surface to remove grime and leave a shiny finish.

"When I wipe around my kitchen surfaces, the walls become stained. Can I prevent this?"

If you don't want tiles, you could fit an upstand. This is usually made of the same material as the worktop, is 10 cm (4 in) high and runs along the wall.

"The sliding doors on my wardrobe keep jamming. Is there anything I can do?"

The vast majority will have runners that can be adjusted. Investigate with a screwdriver.

"How do I stop my shelf brackets from pulling off the wall?"

Use the right fixings. You need wall plugs for solid walls and hollow wall fixings for stud walls.

"How can I stop a shelf bowing in the middle?"

If you can't fit another bracket, screw a batten to the wall under the back edge of the shelf to help support it.

"I have a freestanding shelf unit, but I'm worried it may topple over. How can I secure it in place?"

Simply pop a couple of screws through the back and into the wall (at the top) to hold it stable.

"I have an old flat-pack unit, which has rather wobbly joints that won't tighten any more. How can I strengthen it?"

Tighten it up with joint blocks in inconspicuous places.

"My curtain pole brackets have fallen out of my crumbly old walls. How can I get them to stay up?"

Inject resin (extra hard adhesive) into the hole and fix the bracket in place.

"How do I save electricity?"

1. Fit low-energy light bulbs 2. Don't leave the television on standby. 3. Unplug mobile phone chargers when not in use. 4. Replace old white goods with energy-efficient versions. 5. Turn lights off when you leave a room.

"How do I save water?"

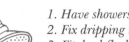

1. *Have showers instead of baths,*
2. *Fix dripping taps immediately.*
3. *Fit dual flush toilet cisterns.*
4. *Run the dishwasher only when it's full.*

"How do I save fuel?"

1. Get your boiler serviced regularly and any other fuel-burning appliances. 2. Insulate your loft, 3. Fit draught excluders.

"How often does my water softener need servicing?"

Once every three years or so, but remember to keep topping it up with salt, once a month on average.

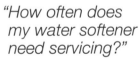

"Do I need carbon monoxide detectors in my home?"

Yes, if you have fuel-burning appliances such as a gas boiler or fire.

"Can I fit a carbon monoxide alarm?"

Yes, they usually just plug into an electric socket.

"I have an electric carbon monoxide alarm, but how do I plug it in at ceiling level? I've got no sockets on my ceiling."

Unlike smoke alarms, carbon monoxide alarms are not used at ceiling level. They are best positioned on a wall (check the manufacturer's recommendations).

"I've been given some little self-adhesive pads that are supposed to detect carbon monoxide. Are they any good?"

Yes, but they only have a limited lifespan. Be sure to write the date on them when first positioned, and check how long before they expire.

"How can I get better reception on my radio?"

Fit an FM aerial in your loft and run the cable downstairs to plug in the back of the radio.

"What do I do if I smell gas?"

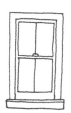

Extinguish naked flames, and turn the gas off at the source. Don't turn electric switches on or off, and open doors and windows. Go outside and telephone the gas emergency service.

"Can I repair or move gas pipes?"

NO. You must employ a properly qualified professional.

"Is it worth getting a fire extinguisher?"

Yes, but you may need two. Water extinguishers can be used for most fires, but a dry powder extinguisher is needed for chip pan and electrical fires.

"What's a fire blanket?"

It's a sheet of non-flammable material that is placed over a small fire to extinguish it. They are commonly used in kitchens as they are ideal for chip pan fires.

"My UPVC windows don't open very far, and I'm worried about escape in the event of a fire. Can they be adjusted?"

Yes. You need to fit egress friction stay hinges, which will allow the window to open much wider.

"We live in an apartment with no fire escape. Is there anything we can do?"

Yes, buy a compact fire escape ladder, which can be hooked over the window sill in the event of a fire.

"What is a fire door?"

A door specially designed to slow down the progress of a fire, with fire-rated hinges, a door closer and intumescent strips around the door edge. These swell up when heated, stopping flames and also possibly smoke.

"How can I make a door more fireproof?"

Use intumescent paint. In the event of a fire, the surface creates a char layer, which insulates the door from the flames.

"I have young children and am worried about them falling out of the upstairs windows. Is there anything I can do?"

Yes, fit window limiter catches to prevent them being opened too far.

"I'm concerned that my glass coffee table is not safe for my children. Should I get rid of it?"

You can buy glass safety film to spread across its surface, which will prevent shards flying everywhere in the event of a breakage.

"How can I stop my son getting into the kitchen cupboard that holds the cleaning products?"

Simply fit a cabinet slide lock, which clamps around both handles.

"My child keeps locking himself in the toilet. We want privacy but also access! Is there an option?"

Yes, fit an emergency release door latch, which allows you to open the door from the other side with a special key.

notes

Renovating

"We're having lots of renovation work done. Do we need to employ a project manager?"

You need someone to run things, so yes, unless the main contractor (builder) is taking on this role.

"Is it realistic to do your own project management on a big build job?"

It's possible, but without experience you'll need a lot of help from your builder or architect.

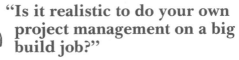

"Do you always need planning permission for new building work?"

No, it depends on many things: the size of the planned extension, whether the building is listed and whether you live in a conservation area, for example. Phone your local planning authority for advice.

"What is a building inspector?"

He checks renovation work to make sure it complies with regulations. Despite what you may hear, they are normally very helpful.

"What's the best advice when getting building estimates and costs?"

Try to get tradesmen to give you fixed prices, rather than estimates. It is best to get at least three quotations for a job.

"How do you find the best tradesmen?"

Always go with personal recommendations.

"Should I have a contract with my builder?"

It's not essential, but the more safeguards you have, the better it is for both parties.

"How should I pay my builder?"

In instalments as the job progresses. This can be weekly or monthly, or when particular stages of the job are complete. Always leave the biggest payment until the end when everything is finished.

"Is it ok to pay a builder a deposit?"

For large jobs yes, as he may need to buy a lot of materials to get the job started.

"Do I need an architect to oversee my renovation?"

For big jobs it can be a good idea, but it is not completely necessary.

"Which one would add more value to my home, a conservatory or an extension?"

Adding extra space will always add value. The extension would normally be more profitable as the space could be used for a whole range of different purposes. It will, however, be more expensive to build.

"We're building an extension. Will we need a bigger boiler?"

Not necessarily. Your existing one may cope, but you'll need to get advice from a heating engineer.

"We want to knock through to make our dining room and kitchen into one space. How do we know what type of beam to use to support the ceiling?"

You may not need one if the wall you are removing is not load-bearing. Get a structural engineer to answer your questions before you begin.

"I'm replacing the old vinyl floor tiles in my kitchen with hard tiles. Can I lay them over the top?"

No, you must remove the vinyl ones first. Try using a spade, as it acts like a giant scraper, lifting tile edges with ease.

"I've taken up my carpet and there are big gaps around the base of the skirting board. How can I repair these?"

Nail some quarter-round beading to the skirting to hang down and cover the gap.

"How do I fit a carpet on a concrete floor as I can't nail the gripper rods around the edge?"

Glue the rods down on a concrete floor rather than trying to nail them.

"Can I lay new carpet on top of the old stuff?"

No, old carpet is a haven for dust and other nasties, so rip it out before laying the new carpet.

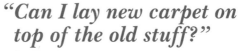

"Can I reuse old carpet underlay?"

If it's in good condition, certainly.

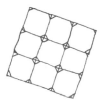

"What sort of floor do I need to lay vinyl on?"

It has to be really flat, so a good concrete screed is best. You can't lay directly on floorboards, so you'll need to cover them with a layer of hardboard or plyboard first.

"Do I need to glue down vinyl flooring?"

Not if it's sheet vinyl. Vinyl tiles need gluing, however. Simply glue around the edges and along any joins.

"What is a floating floor?"

A floating floor is laid with no fixings or adhesive connecting it to the structural floor below. Most laminate floors, for example, are laid in this way.

"Why do I need underlay for my laminate floor?"

It evens out any bumps in the floor below.

"What's the difference between a solid oak floor and an engineered oak floor?"

Solid oak is just oak, whereas engineered oak has an oak top layer stuck on to softwood or man-made board.

"Can I lay a wooden floor if I've got underfloor heating?"

Check with the manufacturer, but most wooden floors should be fine.

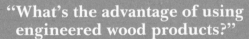

"Is it ok to lay a wooden floor in a bathroom?"

Most manufacturers advise against it because of the moist atmosphere. If you do, make sure it is well coated with varnish to prevent water getting into the surface.

"What's the advantage of using engineered wood products?"

Manufacturers claim that they are less likely to bow or go out of shape. They are also generally cheaper than solid-wood equivalents.

"Is it straightforward to fit new electrical sockets?"

It's very straightforward for an electrician to do the job, and relatively inexpensive.

"Can I wire up my lamps to come on using the switch by the door?"

Certainly, but it is best for an electrician do the work. He will put in a separate circuit to supply the lamps.

"How much lighting do I need?"

Address your 'task' lighting first: this illuminates dark corners and work surfaces, for example. When this is sorted out, consider the 'mood' lighting: where do you need occasional lamps or wall uplighters to provide atmosphere?

"Can I change a single electrical socket for a double?"

Yes, and you can even buy a double converter socket, which simply screws over the top with no wiring required.

"I need some electric wire. Do I buy cable or flex?"

Cable is the wire used for the circuit, and flex is the connection from an appliance or lampholder to the circuit.

"What's the best way of cutting the sheathing off wires, ready for connecting to terminals?"

Wire strippers are specially designed for this purpose.

"I have an old fireplace that I've never used. Is it okay to light a fire?"

No, you should have it checked by a flue specialist first.

"Do all gas fires need a chimney?"

Not any more: it is possible to buy flueless gas fires. All gas fires must be fitted by a fully qualified registered professional.

"Must I be on the mains gas supply to have a gas fire?"

No, with many gas fires you can use bottled gas.

"Can I use MDF to make a plinth under my kitchen units?"

Yes, but make sure that the bottom edge is well painted so it will not absorb moisture when you mop the floor.

"My kitchen is cold and I've got no wall space for radiators. What can I do?"

Fit plinth heaters. As the name suggests, they are cut into the plinth under your kitchen units.

"I'm planning a new kitchen. Where do I start?"

Take specific measurements of all wall lengths, wall heights, window and door positions. Go to a supplier and get them to do the planning for you. They do it all the time and can provide the best advice. Just don't let them get carried away: most people don't need four different types of oven and three wine racks!

"We've got a small cramped kitchen. How can we make a greater impression of space in a new design?"

Use lots of base units for storage and limit the number of wall units. Instead, use open shelving for storage above the worktops.

"We want to move our kitchen from one room to the other side of the house. Is this possible?"

Yes, but bear in mind that kitchens have a lot of electrical and plumbing supplies. For example, make sure that you can fit the necessary waste pipes and drainage for the new kitchen without too much complication and expense.

"Is it best to buy a flat-pack kitchen or one with units already assembled?"

Flat pack is generally cheaper, but you'll spend a lot of time putting the units together. Check the quality of the units in the showroom before you order to help make your decision.

"Do fitted kitchens have standardized unit sizes?"

Generally yes, but the depth of units sometimes varies between manufacturers. Shallower units have less storage space, but it may be easier to run services behind them.

"Can I fit a kitchen myself?"

Most practical people can put together a fitted kitchen. However, it is just as important that you, or your tradesmen, have made sure all the wires and pipes are in the right place.

"I want to fit my new kitchen units. Where do I start?"

Always begin with the corner unit(s).

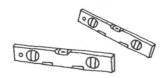

"Should I hang wall units first or get base units in place?"

Start with the base units.

"My walls are very uneven. How can I make sure my kitchen units fit neatly?"

The front edge is the important edge, so make any adjustments along the back. Units can be packed out along the back edge with wedges, or use adjustable angle brackets.

"I've finished putting in my fitted kitchen, but there seem to be lots of fixings and screws left over. Is there something I haven't done?"

Don't worry, as long as you've followed the instructions carefully. Most manufacturers give you extra fixings just in case, so a surplus is perfectly normal.

"Must I make a hole in the wall for my kitchen extractor fan to vent outside?"

Not always. Some can use air circulators and filters that require no exterior outlet.

"Do big fridges with ice dispensers just plug into the wall?"

No, they will need to be plumped into a cold water supply as well.

"How can I integrate an old washing machine into a new kitchen?"

There's nothing to stop you putting it inside a unit carcass and fitting a door to match your new units.

"What's the quickest way of revamping the look of my kitchen?"

Apart from paint, just change the unit drawer and door fronts. If you're on a tight budget, even changing the unit handles will make a difference.

"I need to drill holes in my kitchen unit doors for handles. Is there anything I need to know?"

Yes, make sure you hold an offcut of wood on the back of the door where the drill bit will emerge. This will stop the drill bit splitting the wood. Be sure to keep your hand out of the way of the emerging drill bit!

"The screws that came with the cupboard door handles are too long. Help!"

Handles usually come with screws of two different lengths. If this isn't the case, cut the long ones down with a hacksaw.

"How do I fit the door for an integral fridge?"

They are usually supplied with a special bracket or alternative fixing system. You normally have to put the handle on before you fit the door.

"What's the most hardwearing kitchen worktop?"

They're all pretty good these days. Granite is fairly indestructible, but remember that wooden worktops are straightforward to repair.

"Do all worktops need treating?"

No, usually only wooden ones. Make sure wooden worktops are also treated on the underside before they are fitted.

"How do I cut a hole in a wooden worktop to fit a sink?"

Use the template supplied with the sink to mark a guideline with a pencil. Drill a hole large enough to accommodate a jigsaw blade and cut round the guideline, taking care to support the weight of the section you're cutting out.

"How do I join two lengths of worktop at a corner?"

For granite and synthetic stone, leave it to the professionals who usually include fitting in the price of the worktops. For wood and laminates, the easiest way is to use a joining strip. If you want a perfect join, use a jig and router or call in a professional.

"Is the weight of the worktops simply supported by the kitchen units?"

Yes, although extra support can be added by running a length of 5 x 2.5 cm (2 x 1 in) batten around the wall, level with the tops of the units.

"How far should my worktop overhang the kitchen units?"

It is down to personal preference. Sometimes you may be limited by the depth of the units and worktop so check sizes.

"If we want a breakfast bar, will we have to join lengths of worktop?"

No, as most manufacturers supply extra wide worktops for this purpose.

"Our boiler is very ugly; can we include it in a new kitchen unit, or box it in?"

Take professional advice from a heating engineer. As a guideline, a boiler with a conventional flue needs a good air supply and can be boxed in only if you retain good ventilation. If you have a balanced flue, boxing in is acceptable as long as you leave good access for servicing.

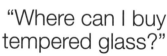

"Where can I buy tempered glass?"

Any 'trade' glass supply outlet will order it for you. Be sure to take accurate measurements of what you require.

"Our new conservatory is too hot in the summer and too cold in the winter. Any tips?"

If you don't want to bother with radiators and blinds, fit an air conditioning unit to deal with seasonal changes effectively.

"How can I soundproof my room?"

Lay soundproofing slabs below your carpet (like a thick heavy underlay). For walls and ceilings, you'll need to use soundproofing quilt or acoustic slabs. These have to be fitted as part of a new wall/ceiling structure. This is perfectly possible, but you'll need professional advice.

"Can I soundproof a door?"

You can buy strips that fit along the bottom edge of a door, that open and close automatically with the door.

"How can I soundproof my windows?"

Double glazing is effective, but introducing another layer of glazing on the inside will improve things even more (effectively triple glazing). This system takes the form of sliding glass panels, which fit in a frame in the internal window reveals.

"Can I convert a regular door into a sliding door?"

Yes, but you'll need to buy a sliding door kit, and make a number of adjustments to the existing door and frame.

"I've taken out a doorway as I want an arch. What's the simplest way to make one?"

Buy and fit an arch former, which can be made from plaster or mesh. Mesh formers have greater adjustment capabilities.

"Can I convert a flat-faced door to a panel door?"

Yes, buy a selection of self-adhesive panels and stick them to the surface of the door.

"How many hinges should I put on a door?"

Three is best and essential for exterior doors. Two will suffice on good-quality interior doors.

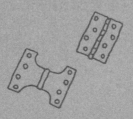

"How do I know where to position hinges?"

The top edge of the top hinge should be 15 cm (6 in) down from the top of the door. The bottom edge of the bottom hinge should be 23 cm (9 in) up from the bottom of the door. If you have a third hinge, it goes mid way between the other two.

"Are there different qualities of hinge?"

Yes. In many circumstances it's a choice of cost and appearance. However, fire doors must have special fire-rated hinges.

"I want my doors to close automatically, but don't want one of those ugly things you stick on the frame. Are there any other options?"

Concealed door closers can be fitted along the hinging edge of the door.

"We want to fit new double-glazed windows, but don't want plastic ones. Are there any other options?"

Yes, double glazed doesn't mean UPVC; you can get wooden or metal windows, or different combinations of these, and still have double glazing.

"Why are there small vents along the top edges of my windows, and can I get rid of them?"

They're called trickle vents, and no you shouldn't get rid of them, as they provide ventilation. They can, however, be closed.

"We want new wooden windows. Should we choose hardwood or softwood?"

Hardwood is better and will last longer, but the windows will be more expensive.

"Can I convert a wooden single-glazed window into a double-glazed one?"

It depends how deep the glazing bars are, as a double-glazed glass unit is much thicker than a single sheet of glass.

"Which is the best type of window lock?"

This depends on the window design. New windows can be made with excellent security features (locking points along the edges that work with the latch), so try to specify this if you're having some made. For older windows, there is a wide selection to choose from, so spend a little more to make sure you are buying quality.

"Is triple glazing even more efficient than double glazing?"

Probably...but the jury is still out. Good double glazing is pretty efficient!

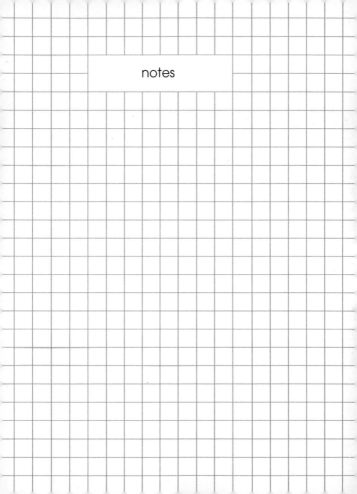

notes

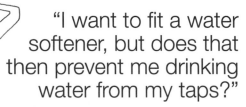

"I want to fit a water softener, but does that then prevent me drinking water from my taps?"

Yes and no. You should not drink softened water, but a water softener can be installed to by-pass the kitchen tap so you still have a source of drinking water.

"Is a water softener the only way to reduce limescale?"

No, there are magnetic and electrolytic scale inhibitors too. These are cheaper to install, and are designed only to reduce the scale, not soften the water. They are, perhaps, not so effective as water softeners.

"*Are waste disposal units a good idea?*"

It's down to personal preference: some people swear by them, others can't stand them. If you do fit one, be sure to have lots of rodding points in the waste pipe system, as they are prone to blocking (usually because people don't use them correctly!).

"I'd love an old-fashioned roll-top bath, but they're so expensive. Is there an alternative?"

Yes, manufacturers are now making acrylic versions that are both cheaper and lighter.

"Can I fit a toilet in my basement?"

Yes, but there could be a problem with the waste pipe as it may not be able to drain downwards. In order to get the waste out, you may need to fit a macerator to pump waste up into the drainage system.

"What is the advantage of a dual-fuel towel rail?"

They come on with your heating in the winter, but in the summer (or when heating is off) they are powered by a separate electric supply, which can be fitted with a timer.

"Do basins always need a pedestal?"

No, some can be wall mounted, but the basin must be designed for this purpose and you will need strong wall fixings.

"I'm fitting a new basin; do I fit the taps (faucets) first or last?"

Always fit the taps and the waste to the basin before you fix the basin into its final position, as you will have better access.

"I want a wall-mounted basin, but am worried that the ugly pipes below will ruin the effect. What can I do?"

Use a chrome waste rather than a standard waste, as it's much more decorative.

"How do I wall hang a toilet?"

They come with a special mounting frame for the purpose.

"How do I ensure my walls are strong enough for wall-mounted bathroom fittings?"

Block walls are usually fine. If you have stud walls, make sure that there is studwork (solid timber) in the areas where the fixings will be. Plan for this eventuality if you are building a new stud wall.

"How can I save space in my small bathroom?"

Fit a space-saving toilet, which can be fitted in the corner.

"I have a tiny shower room. How can I stop it getting all misty?"

You must have an extractor fan. If it is a very small room, you can buy extractor fans that are combined with light fittings.

"What is the advantage of fitting a water softener?"

If you live in an area with hard water, the softener will greatly reduce limescale, so lengthening the life of boilers and washing machines, for example. It also makes soap lather better.

"I'm fitting a shower tray, but the waste seems to be too big to fit underneath. Help!"

Try a shallow bottle trap for the waste, or cut a hole in the floor to accommodate the waste system.

"People keep telling me electric showers are easy to fit. Why?"

Because they only require a cold water supply (although they also need an electric supply).

"How should I fix a shower tray in place?"

Solid trays should sit on a bed of mortar, while plastic trays have feet that are held in place with screws.

"Is it always possible to have a shower fitted?"

Yes, but the type will depend on your water system. There are three main types of shower: standard mixers, pumped showers and electric showers.

"Because bathrooms get so damp, do I need to use special wood for skirting boards?"

No, just make sure they are well painted. However, it is a good idea to use moisture-resistant MDF for bath panels, or anywhere that is constantly splashed with water.

"Is it complicated to plumb in new taps (faucets)?"

As long as you know how to turn off the water, it's fairly straightforward. Using flexible tap connectors makes life a lot easier as there is no need for soldered connections.

"Is a hacksaw the best tool for cutting copper pipes?"

No, use a pipe cutter as you get a much cleaner cut.

"What's the most cost-effective way of putting in a new bathroom?"

Don't change the positions of the different elements so you don't need any new pipework.

"We're selling our house. Would it be a good idea to put in a new bathroom to help the sale. What do you suggest?"

Buy a simple white suite. Spend a little extra on taps to give it a more luxurious look.

"We're having a new boiler; do we also have to replace the heating pipes?"

Not necessarily, although if you are changing to a pressurized system, you should get the existing pipes, pressure tested to check they can cope.

"Can plastic pipes be used for a new heating system?"

Yes, as long as the manufacturer specifies they are suitable.

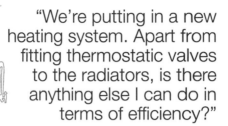

"We're putting in a new heating system. Apart from fitting thermostatic valves to the radiators, is there anything else I can do in terms of efficiency?"

Fit room thermostats too, as these prevent the heating system starting if room temperatures are already satisfactory. Otherwise the heating comes on just for the radiator thermostats to tell it to close down again.

"Why has underfloor heating become so popular?"

It provides a nice, consistent heat and you don't need to have ugly radiators on your walls.

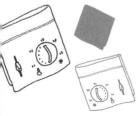

"Are there different types of underfloor heating?"

There are two main types: wet systems with hot water pipes under the floor, and dry systems with electric cables under the floor.

"Is underfloor heating straightforward to fit?"

In a new extension or for a new-build property, yes. In an existing property, it means big upheaval. On a smaller scale, it's perfectly possible to fit an electric system in a bathroom, for example.

"Are there any drawbacks to underfloor heating?"

Apart from the expense, it is not possible to have relatively quick changes in temperature: it's always gradual.

"What is the best way of insulating a loft?"

Blanket insulation is still the quickest, most efficient method and cheapest.

"What depth of insulation do I need in a loft?"

For standard blanket insulation, the recommend depth is at least 27 cm (10½ in).

"A friend told me I have to lay some sort of membrane before rolling out loft insulation. Is this true?"

Yes, you should lay a thin plastic membrane between joists to stop any moist air coming through from the rooms below.

"How do I stop getting all itchy when laying insulation?"

Make sure you wear a dust mask, gloves and goggles. Also, wear a throwaway set of overalls – they're really cheap and very effective.

"Can I lay insulation over the top of light fittings?"

No, cut a hole around them so they don't overheat.

"Can I insulate over electrical cables?"

It is better to lift them carefully above the insulation to prevent the risk of overheating.

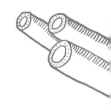

"What's the best way of insulating water pipes?"

Custom-made pipe insulation, which is cut down its length to allow it to wrap straight round the pipe.

"How do I join lengths of pipe insulation?"

Butt lengths tightly together and tape them in place.

"We're converting our loft space. How do I insulate the sloping roof?"

There are many options, including blanket insulation, board insulation and modern foil insulation. What you use depends on the depth of the rafters, local codes of practice and what type of roofing felt you have. It is all rather complicated, so get professional advice.

"How can I make more storage space in our converted loft?"

Build low walls close to the eaves, and make simple hatch access to these areas.

"I want to convert our loft to another bedroom. How do I know if it's possible?"

You generally need 2 m (6½ ft) of headroom to make it possible. There are strict guidelines relating to fire escapes and insulation needs, so you will need professional guidance.

"We live in a small apartment. How can we gain extra space?"

If you have high ceilings, consider a mezzanine floor as you can literally double your floor area. On a smaller scale, simply putting a child's bed on a raised platform in a bedroom gives extra space underneath.

"Can all cavity walls be insulated?"

Cavity wall insulation is a good idea but is not always recommended, so speak to a specialist.

"How is cavity wall insulation fitted?"

Holes are drilled in the outer wall and it is blown in.

"I want to buy an electric drill, but don't know which one to buy. Help!"

The most useful is a cordless drill/screwdriver with a hammer action to help drill into masonry walls. For a lot of heavy-duty work, get an SDS (special drive system) drill.

"Do all drill bits fit all drills?"

No, there are two categories: standard drill bits and SDS drill bits.

"How do I know how far to drill into a wall for a particular fixing?"

Hold the fixing next to the drill bit and mark its length on the bit with a piece of tape. Drill into the wall until you reach the taped part of the bit.

"How do I stop my drill bit sliding across the wall surface when it starts up?"

It comes with practice, but start by making a small indent in the wall surface with a hammer and punch at the point you wish to make the hole.

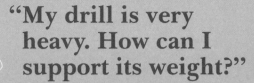

"My drill is very heavy. How can I support its weight?"

Check in the carry case to see if it has a support handle. If there isn't one, you can support the weight by holding your hand under the main body of the drill.

"When should I use the 'hammer action' on my new drill?"

Only when drilling into masonry.

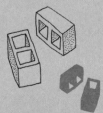

"Nearly every time I try to hammer in a nail, the head of the hammer 'slips' off the nail. What am I doing wrong?"

Cleaning the head (face) of the hammer with sandpaper should stop this happening.

"How can I saw in a straight line?"

Draw a pencil guideline and have the angle of the blade at 45° to the wood. Look down over the top of the blade, while you saw and make sure the section of wood is securely clamped.

"After I've started sawing, the blade seems to get stuck. How can I stop this happening?"

Keeping the blade straight will help this problem. Also, once the cut is established, position a wedge at the beginning of the cut to hold it open a little.

"If you have the choice, is it best to saw across the grain or with the grain?"

It's always easiest to saw across the grain.

"How do I stop wood moving about while I saw it?"

Buy a workbench, which allows you to clamp the wood firmly. Also, employ a helper to hold large pieces of wood.

"How do I cut a curve in a piece of wood?"

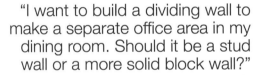

An electric jigsaw is a great tool for this. Make sure you have the right blade for the type of wood you are cutting.

"I want to build a dividing wall to make a separate office area in my dining room. Should it be a stud wall or a more solid block wall?"

Stud is much lighter, which is especially important if you are building upstairs. You also need good bricklaying skills to build a block wall.

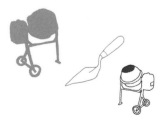

"What is dry lining?"

This is a modern alternative to plastering, where plaster-based wall boards are used as the decorative surface (rather than the wall being plastered over before decoration). Joints between boards are taped, filled (with a special compound) and honed flat with the surrounding board area.

"Is plastering a DIY job?"

With lots of practice, but if you don't have time, get the professionals in.

"What size timbers should I use when building a stud wall?"

A non-structural stud wall can be built from 100 x 50 mm (4 x 2 in) or 75 x 50 mm (3 x 2 in) timber.

"How far apart should I position vertical studs?"

Space the studs at 40 cm (16 in) if you are using 9.5 mm (⅜ in) thick plasterboard; or 60 cm (2 ft) if you are using 12.5 mm (½ in) thick plasterboard.

"Are the studs in stud walls always made from timber?"

No, stud walls can be constructed using metal channels attached to floors and ceilings, which slot together to make a frame for the wall.

"Do I need any horizontal timbers in a stud wall?"

Apart from the head plate along the ceiling and the floor plate along the floor, cut and fit short sections of timber (noggins) between the vertical studs about halfway between ceiling and floor.

"Should I nail or screw the studs together when making a stud wall?"

You have the choice, but you will have greater control with screws.

"I want to make a stud wall with metal supports. How do I join the metal sections together?"

In some places they will slot together, in others use small drywall screws.

"What do I use to cut the sections for a metal stud wall?"

You can use a hacksaw, but tin snips are by far the best tool.

"Does a door frame fit directly into a metal stud wall?"

Yes, but the frame around it is strengthened with timber first.

"I've built the frame of my metal stud wall, but it doesn't seem very robust. Is it going to be ok?"

Don't worry: the plasterboard will strengthen everything and make a very solid structure.

"I want to dryline my new wall. What plasterboard should I use to cover it?"

The sheets must have tapered edges, rather than square ones. The joints between boards are then taped and filled flush with the main board surface.

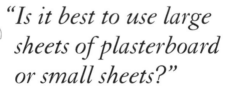

"Is it best to use large sheets of plasterboard or small sheets?"

Large sheets cover the area quicker, but small sheets (laths) are much easier to handle. If you're drylining, you must use large sheets.

"I'm plasterboarding a ceiling. How do I hold the sheets in position when fixing them up?"

You'll certainly need two people, but you can also hire a special board lifter, which lifts and holds sheets at ceiling level, making it much easier to fix them in place.

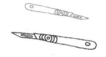

"What's the best way of cutting plasterboard?"

Use an old saw, or score a line with a craft knife and 'snap' the board.

"Why is my plasterboard green on one side?"

It means it has some moisture resistance and so it is ideal for bathrooms. Pink plasterboard denotes that it has been fire proofed.

"Should I nail or screw the sheets of plasterboard to the studs when making 'a stud wall'?"

It's personal choice. Nails are cheaper but you might dent boards if you're not accurate with hammer blows. If you use screws, they must be drywall screws.

"How many nails do I need to fix each plasterboard sheet when making a stud wall?"

Use a nail or drywall screw every 15 cm (6 in).

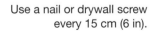

"Do I need to cover the joints between plasterboard sheets before they are plastered?"

Yes, use plasterer's scrim tape; self-adhesive tape is easiest to use. If you're drylining, apply drylining tape before it is filled over.

"Help, I've got some rather large gaps around the edge where my plasterboard wasn't cut exactly to size. Should I cut another sheet?"

Not necessarily: if your gaps are larger than 3 mm (⅛ in), use plaster bonding coat to fill the gaps flush with the board surface. Bonding coat is just powder mixed with water: like a filler, but much stickier.

"I'm building a block wall to make a downstairs toilet. How do I join it to the existing walls?"

Use wall profiles. These metal strips are screwed to the existing wall. Wall ties are attached to the profiles and fit between the courses of your new wall.

"Can I build a block wall on a wooden floor?"

Yes, but you must be sure that the floor is strong enough. It would be better to build a stud wall, which is much lighter.

"What do I use to support the blocks in a wall above a door?"

You'll need a concrete lintel to span the opening.

"How do I cut concrete blocks?"

With a club hammer and bolster chisel, or an angle grinder.

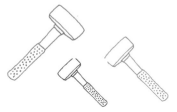

"Do block walls have to be rendered before they are plastered?"

No, plasterboard can be fixed to them. Attach the board to wooden battens on the wall, or use a strong adhesive to bond the plasterboard directly to the blocks.

"Does plaster coving need to be nailed in place?"

Coving is usually fixed with adhesive, but nails can be used to add temporary support while the adhesive dries. They may then be removed, or left in place if you make sure their heads are punched below the coving surface and covered over with filler.

"I want to block up an old doorway. How can I do this?"

If it's a solid block or brick wall, it's best to use blocks. For a stud wall, use a stud framework. Using similar materials helps prevent any cracking in the finished surface.

"Is it straightforward to knock a doorway through into another room?"

Yes, but you must first establish whether it is a load-bearing wall. This will determine what temporary support you need while making the hole. Get professional advice.

"Are stud walls always non-load-bearing?"

NO.

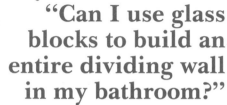

"Can I use glass blocks to build an entire dividing wall in my bathroom?"

Yes, but it will definitely need metal reinforcing rods to maintain its structure.

"Can I use normal mortar for a glass block wall?"

You can, but it's much more attractive to use a white mortar.

"How do I keep the mortar joints even in a glass block wall?"

Use spacers provided by the manufacturer.

"Do I have to use mortar when building a glass block wall?"

No, you can build it dry using a wooden frame supplied by the manufacturer.

"Can I use a glass block wall to form part of a shower cubicle?"

Yes, but the mortar must be waterproof. Be sure to seal around the edges with silicone sealant.

"How do I go round corners with coving?"

You need a mitre block to cut the corners accurately. Some manufacturers provide a template for cutting the mitred (mitered) cuts for both internal and external corners.

"How do I fix a plaster ceiling rose to the ceiling?"

Use coving adhesive and screw fixings. You'll need to drill pilot holes in the ceiling rose first. Use a joist detector to find good fixing points.

"I want a textured ceiling with plain coving, but which do I do first?"

It is usual to fit the coving first, followed by the textured ceiling coating.

"How do I make the patterns in a textured coating?"

The most common tool to use is a stippling brush, but manufacturers provide other tools to create different effects.

"How do I finish off around the edges when creating a textured ceiling?"

Run a 2.5 cm (1 in) brush around the edges of the design to create a neat frame effect. Simply dampen the brush with water and drag it through the coating.

"We want to change our old skirting boards for a new style. What is the easiest way of getting the old stuff off?"

Ease it away with a pry bar or a claw hammer.

"How do I fix skirting board to the wall?"

Ideally nail it, using masonry nails for solid walls and wire nails if you're nailing into the studs on a stud wall.

"My nails won't hold my skirting board in place. Help!"

Use screws and/or apply some grab adhesive along the back of the board to help stick it to the wall.

"Why do I keep splitting skirting boards when I try fixing them to the wall?"

You are inserting fixings too near the edge of the board, or too close to the ends of the lengths.

"How do I deal with corners when fitting skirting?"

You need a mitre (miter) saw to cut accurate 45° joins for adjacent sections.

"What's the best way of making sure a mitre (miter) join on an external corner doesn't split open?"

On external corners (ones that point into the room), pilot drill two holes across the joint and insert two nails or small screws to hold it secure. Applying some wood glue along the joint as it is assembled will also help.

"How do I join two lengths of skirting board on a straight section of wall?"

Rather than butt straight edges together, which is likely to crack in time, make a 45° joint between the lengths.

"Should I fit architraves around doorways before the skirting boards, or vice versa?"

Architraves first, as the skirting then butts up to them.

"What's the best way to fix a wooden dado rail to the wall?"

Treat it like skirting board: use masonry nails for solid walls and wire nails on a stud wall.

"How do I panel my walls using tongue and groove?"

First you must fix 5 x 2.5 cm (2 x 1 in) battens on the wall surface, providing a fixing wall framework. The battens should lie at 90° to the direction in which the tongue and groove will run. Next, fix the tongue and groove planks against the battens and nail through the tongue into the batten at 45°.

"If I want to panel a wall, what do I do with the radiators?"

You need to take the radiators off temporarily, panel the wall, then refit them. Unless you're a competent plumber, get professional help, as the pipes will probably now need to be moved forwards.

"Is a tongue and groove panel system suitable for a ceiling?"

Yes, but you will still need to fix a framework of 5 x 2.5 cm (2 x 1 in) battens on the ceiling on which to nail the tongue and groove.

"We hate our stair banisters. Is there a way of changing them without replacing the whole staircase?"

Yes, manufacturers provide replacement balustrade kits for just this purpose.

"How can we make our staircase look more modern?"

Staircase structure is governed by many safety regulations, so there's not much you can do to an existing staircase apart from changing the handrail. You may need to consider finding a bespoke manufacturer to come up with a contemporary new design.

"We'd love to fit a spiral staircase in our home. Is it best to buy reclaimed or new?"

You may find an old one that you like, but consider how you are going to get it into your house, especially if it doesn't break down into small sections. Many manufacturers produce self-assembly spiral staircase kits, which are straightforward to put together and don't create trouble with access.

"Is solar energy a real choice for the average home owner?"

It certainly is and solar panel design and efficiency improves all the time. If you're upgrading your heating system, consider solar, as it could reduce your energy bills and is a very green option.

"Can I have a wind turbine on my house?"

In most cases, you'll need planning permission. Like solar energy, efficiency with new technology is always improving so carry out plenty of research before you commit to a specific system.

"What's the single most important thing to do if I want to make my home greener?"

Insulate, especially your loft. It saves you money and saves energy.

"Is it true that paper is sometimes used as insulation?"

Yes, recycled shredded paper is commonly blown into wall or attic spaces.

"Is there a greener alternative to using that itchy blanket insulation?"

Sheeps' wool is a good alternative.

"What reclaimed products can we use when renovating our home?"

There are plenty of options. Some examples are floorboards, bricks, fireplaces, beams, radiators, baths and tiles.

"What are the problems with reclaimed materials?"

You need to check for damage, and accept that some things may need repair. There also tends to be a lot of wastage with floorboards, for example, as some may be split or damaged beyond repair.

"How do I know if new wood has come from a sustainable source?"

See if it has been stamped by a recognized association that promotes sustainable forestry.

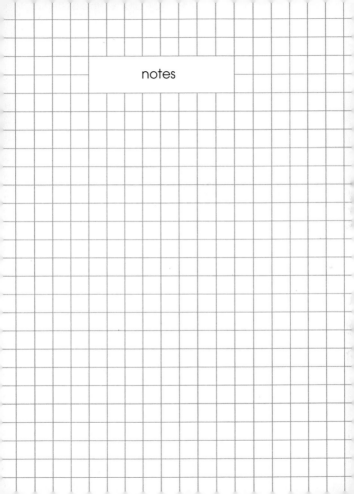

notes

Decorating

& tiling

"Where should I start if I am going to re-decorate?"

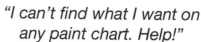

Create a theme board and pin fabric swatches, including different textures and patterns, and magazine clippings of room features and furniture you like.

"The swatches supplied by painting and decorating stores are so small. How can I get a better idea of how a paint will look?"

Buy tester pots and paint pieces of lining paper, which may then be moved around the room to check how it will work in all lights.

"I can't find what I want on any paint chart. Help!"

Find it elsewhere. Many suppliers can scan items and produce a paint to match that is tailor-made to your own requirements.

"I want to transform my living room completely. Where do I begin?"

One way is to pick a one or two items in the room and build a scheme around it.

"I'm about to start painting my living room. Where do I start?"

Prepare surfaces and prime any wood, then work from the top down: ceilings, walls then woodwork.

"Are cotton or plastic dust sheets best?"

Cotton sheets are better on floors as plastic is slippery. Thin plastic is ideal for covering furniture.

"I'm confused: what's the difference between gloss, satin and eggshell paints?"

It's all in the finish they give. Gloss is very shiny, satin is mid-sheen and eggshell is nearly matt.

"How do I fill a hole in a wall?"

Use powder filler mixed to a paste with water. You can also use a tub of ready mixed filler but, it's more expensive.

"How do I fill a large crack between my wall and skirting board?"

Roll up some newspaper and wedge in the gap to provide a base for some filler.

"How can I stop my dust sheets from creeping across the floor as I work?"

Secure them to the floor with masking tape.

"Is there an easy way to clean a ceiling before painting?"

Use a squeegee mop, which means you don't need a ladder.

"Why do my brushes keep leaving bristles in my paintwork?"

It's normal for a new brush to lose a few bristles, but if it continues, you've obviously bought a very cheap brush! Before use, flick the bristles against the palm of your hand to shed any loose ones.

"What's the difference between a pure bristle brush and a synthetic one?"

Pure bristle brushes are good all-rounders, the best being made from the neck hair of Chinese hogs (yes, really). Synthetic brushes have man-made filaments suitable for water-based paints.

"Can I paint on top of wet filler?"

No. Let it dry, sand it smooth, then paint.

"I keep filling the nail heads in my ceiling, but the filler keeps popping out. What's going on?"

The nails need to be tapped in a bit further using a nail punch. Then refill and sand.

"What is plastic wood?"

It's a quick-drying, very hard filler designed for wood.

"Plastic wood is really hard to sand. Is there a trick I'm missing?"

Yes, it is very hard, that's why it's good. Buy an electric palm sander as it makes easy work of plastic wood and other sanding jobs.

"It takes me ages to sand my walls after filling them. How can I speed up?"

It's always most awkward in corners and tight spaces, so remove excess filler here with a damp sponge before it dries. There is then less to sand!

"Dust appears throughout the house when I'm sanding down. How can I stop this?"

Open the window, close the door and apply masking tape around the edge of the door to stop dust escaping.

"Why do I need primer?"

It seals bare surfaces as a foundation for further coats of paint.

"Can I use all paints inside and outside?"

No. Some can be used for both, but others will specify for interior or exterior use only.

"I always get paint all over my hands and then the phone goes. Help!"

Use disposable latex gloves when painting. You'll never spend hours washing your hands at the kitchen sink again.

"Big tubs of paint are so heavy and difficult to take up a stepladder. What do I do?"

Transfer the paint into a small paint kettle (paint pot). This solves the weight problem and stops the main tub of paint getting contaminated with bits off the brush.

"I have an external corner with a large chip in the plaster, but when I try to fill it the filler falls out. What should I do?"

Temporarily nail a small length of batten down the corner edge, fill up to the batten, let it dry, remove the batten and repeat on the adjacent wall.

"How many coats of paint do I use on my walls?"

Two coats of emulsion is the norm, but three maybe needed for a major change; for instance from mid-blue to off-white.

"Can I paint damp walls?"

No, the damp problem must be solved before paint is applied. For minor damp, you can seal the surface with a two-part resin-based sealer before painting.

"Paint smells terrible. Is there anything I can do?"

Make sure windows and doors are open, and for large surfaces always use water-based paints. You can also buy a respirator mask.

"How much paint do I put on my brush?"

Dip the brush in the paint up to a quarter of the way up the bristles, or a little more for water-based paints.

"Do I always need undercoat?"

No, it's used to create a good foundation for oil-based paints.

"I am painting a large area and will need several cans of paint. How do I ensure a consistent result?"

When you need more than one can of paint, mix them together first in a large container in case there is a slight difference.

"I want to use some old paint, but it is full of bits. Can I save it?"

Yes, stretch an old pair of tights across a paint kettle (small pot) and pour the old paint through the tights to sieve it.

"What is sugar soap and why do I need it?"

It's a powdered soap that is mixed with water and used to wash down surfaces before decorating. It removes grease and grime.

"I keep getting covered in paint when I roller my ceiling. Is there anything I can do to stop this?"

Fit a roller guard: it's like a mud guard for your roller.

"I want to paint my skirting board, but how do I keep splashes off the carpet?"

Run masking tape on the carpet around the base of the skirting board, using a filler knife or scraper to ensure it is pushed right down in the junction.

"I've painted my walls but I can still see the filled areas through the paint surface. What can I do?"

Always prime the filler before painting. You'll need to give it another coat.

"Which paint should I use on new plaster?"

Any emulsion will do, but if the walls are very dusty, apply a coat of diluted emulsion made from 1 part water to 10 parts paint.

"Which paint should I use on my new textured ceiling?"

Emulsion, but first use a broom to knock off any loose bits.

"How can I get rid of my old textured ceiling?"

If it's not too crumbly and loose, it can be plastered over without a problem, but you'll need a professional to do the job.

"I have cracks that keep coming back in my ceiling. How can I get rid of them once and for all?"

Use self-adhesive plasterers' scrim over the cracks, then apply a wide band of filler over the top and sand the edges smooth before painting.

"Can I paint over wallpaper?"

Strictly speaking, no, but if you're sure it is well stuck down and the surface isn't shiny, yes.

"Can you paint directly on new drylined walls?"

You should use a drylining primer first, otherwise you can get a patchy finish.

"Why are some paints cheaper than others?"

It's normally down to quality. There is more pigment in expensive paint, and it tends to be thicker which means you will need fewer coats.

"Are paint pads any good?"

It's purely personal preference. Pads are the direct alternative to a roller.

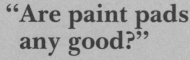

"Stirring large tins of paint takes a long time. How can I speed it up?"

You can buy a paint stirrer attachment for your cordless drill. Make sure you clean it well after use.

"I've just painted over my wallpaper and bubbles are appearing everywhere. Help!"

As long as the bubbles weren't there before painting, don't panic. When the paint dries, most of the bubbles will disappear. Any that remain can be sliced open with a craft knife and stuck down with PVA.

"Can I paint copper heating pipes?"

No problem. Use two coats of emulsion or, for the best finish, use an undercoat and a coat of oil-based gloss or eggshell.

"My house has 12 flush doors. What's the quickest way to paint them?"

Use a mini roller for the main surfaces and a 25 mm (1 in) brush for the edges.

"The joint between my skirting boards and the wall keeps cracking. How can I stop this?"

Use flexible filler, often called caulk. Squeeze it on like silicone sealant and wipe it smooth. Unlike silicone sealant, caulk can be painted.

"How do I get crisp, straight lines when I paint?"

For a start, paint the ceiling overlapping on to the walls and allow it to dry before painting the walls. Similarly, paint the walls to overlap the woodwork before painting the wood. This means you only do one straight line between two surfaces. Use a good brush with bristles of an even length.

"I've got round yellow stains on my woodwork. What's gone wrong?"

The knots in the wood are discolouring the paint. Apply a shellac solution to seal them before repainting.

"Even though I sanded them smooth, my window sills are still gritty after I've painted them. Any ideas for next time?"

Just before painting, wipe down woodwork with kitchen towel dampened with white spirit. This removes dust, and evaporates quickly to leave a perfect painting surface.

"I keep getting drips when I gloss my doors. How do I stop the paint dripping?"

Use less paint on your brush. Also, after you've finished, go away for half an hour then come back and remove any drips that have formed using a dry brush.

"How do I paint areas without getting streaks?"

Use a large brush, 10 cm (4 in) is ideal, applying the paint in one direction first, before lightly 'laying off' at right angles to the first application. Just let the tips of the bristles glide over the paint surface.

"I would like to paint an accent wall in my dining room. Any suggestions?"

Whatever your taste dictates, but bear in mind the simple rule that darker tones will 'advance', making the room seem smaller and cosier, and lighter tones will 'recede', making the room seem larger and airier.

"My ceiling keeps cracking around the edge, however much I fill the gap. How can I solve this?"

Use flexible filler or consider putting up coving.

"I've used a roller to paint my walls and a brush to do the edges, but I can see a line where the brush has been. How can I get rid of this?"

It's important to keep a wet edge, so paint one wall at a time, ensuring that you do the edges while the main rolled area is still wet.

"My son wants a blackboard in his bedroom, and I've seen some blackboard paint. How do I use it?"

Create a border with masking tape, apply two coats of the paint inside the border and remove the masking tape when the paint is dry. An instant blackboard!

"I want to paint my child's new cot. Can I do this?"

Yes, but use child-friendly paint.

"How can I jazz up some old pine shelves?"

Fix some chunky decorative beading along the front edge and paint them to match your decorative scheme.

"How do I paint my wood-burning stove?"

Paint it when it is cold using a heat-resistant paint.

"My son wants yellow and blue stripes painted on his wall. How do I do this?"

Paint the wall yellow first, then use low-tack masking tape to mark off the stripes. Paint the blue stripes and remove the tape to reveal perfect straight edges.

"How do I paint in inaccessible areas, like the narrow space between two light switches?"

Use a fitch, which is a small, long-handled paint brush similar in shape to an artist's paintbrush.

"I have a minimalist kitchen, and don't want to use tiles above my worktops. How can I keep the walls clean?"

Apply two coats of an oil-based eggshell on the splash-back area.

"Must I keep washing out my rollers and brushes? It takes such a long time."

You can keep rollers and brushes perfectly workable for a few days by keeping them closely wrapped in clingfilm (plastic wrap).

"How do I dispose of paint safely?"

You should always take the leftovers to a local authority disposal unit.

"When I'm sanding woodwork, it hurts my fingers. Is there any way to avoid this?"

Wrapping the sandpaper around a block of wood will be more comfortable.

"I have very old crumbly walls that have been wallpapered. What's the best way to get them ready for painting?"

If the wallpaper is well stuck down, you can paint straight on top. Alternatively, hang lining paper first to get a better surface.

"I've just lined my room ready for painting, but I've noticed some gaps between the joins in the paper. What can I do?"

Use a fine surface filler to fill the gaps.

"The paintwork in The walls in my bathroom are always damp. What can I do?"

Use a resistent paint and get an electrician to fix a good extractor fan.

"I want to varnish my new wooden shelves but I can't find a tinted varnish that I like. Have I got any other options?"

Yes, you can use wood dye, which comes in lots of different shades and may also be mixed for further variation. You can then use a clear matt or gloss varnish over the top to protect the surface.

"Why can't I get a good finish with wood stain? I can see brush marks everywhere!"

You're applying too much at a time and not brushing it out enough. Also, if you overlap wet stain on to dry it will show, so always keep a wet edge.

"My ceiling is stained because we had a shower leak above. The leak is now fixed, but when I paint over the stain it keeps coming back. Help!"

You can seal the stain with a coat of oil-based undercoat, before applying a water-based emulsion over the top.

"Why can I see where I have touched up marks on my living room wall?"

Because all paint will fade over time and new dabs (even using the same paint) will be obvious. It's always best to paint the entire wall when touching up.

"My ceiling is all flaky. Can I paint straight over it?"

No. You must scrape off all the loose bits using a scraper or filling knife, and wash it down to remove the dust.

"It's exhausting painting ceilings. Is there any easier way?"

Use a roller and be sure to have an extension attachment for it. This means you don't have to keep getting up and down a ladder. It's also great for walls.

"When I paint my windows frames, I keep getting paint on the glass. Is there a way to avoid this?"

A steady hand, but in the meantime don't worry too much as you can remove dried paint splashes from the glass using a window scraper, or place lengths of masking tape on the glass where it meets the frame. Peel off when the paint is dry.

"How can I stop my metal windows sticking?"

There's probably a big paint build-up on the hinges and the hinged edge. Strip it back to bare metal before repainting.

"My old radiators are so big and ugly. What can I do to disguise them?"

Paint them to match the walls: this way will lessen their presence. Otherwise use radiator covers to hide them.

"Which paint can I use to paint my radiators?"

Eggshell or gloss is best, but paint them cold, and prime any rusty areas with a metal primer first.

"How do I paint my old-fashioned radiators when I can't get a brush into all the gaps?"

Use two or three coats of a water-based aerosol paint (which will dry quicker than an oil-based paint). Be sure to put some newspaper behind the radiator to protect the wall and wear a respirator mask.

"How can I paint behind my radiator?"

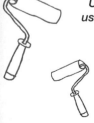

Use a radiator roller or brush. These are also useful for pushing wallpaper behind radiators.

"My small children always leave dirty handprints on the walls when they climb the stairs, but I don't want to keep painting the whole stairwell. Is there another solution?"

Vinyl paints always wipe down well. Alternatively, fit a dado rail about 1 m (1 yard) above the stairs, so that when you redecorate you only need to repaint the area below the rail.

"How can I disguise my uneven walls?"

If you don't want to hang textured or heavily patterned wallpaper, choose darker tones when painting as these always provide better camouflage.

"Can I paint over the top of varnish?"

Yes, but sand it thoroughly first to give it a key.

"I've fitted some new wooden worktops in my kitchen. What should I protect them with?"

You must use oil or wax oil specifically for worktops. Wooden worktop oils are hardwearing and hygienic, but they need regular recoating once or twice a year.

"My kitchen units look tired. Can I paint them?"

Yes, but most will require a coat of specially designed primer (readily available) before paint is applied.

"How do I get a distressed paint finish on my kitchen dresser?"

Paint it one colour and allow to dry, before randomly masking the edges of panels and handles using petroleum jelly. Apply the next colour, allow it to dry, then rub off the areas where the jelly was applied.

"Can I paint a wooden chest of drawers with emulsion?"

Yes, but once you have finished, give it a coat of matt varnish to provide a good protective surface.

"When I'm painting my stairwell, the top of the ladder keeps marking the wall. What can I do to stop this?"

Wrap some cloth pads around the ladder tops, securing them with masking tape.

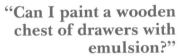

"Why has my paint gone all wrinkly?"

You're probably using gloss and have applied it before the coat below has dried. You'll have to strip it all off and recoat.

"How can I keep paint off the wall when I'm painting pipes?"

Hold a piece of card between the pipes and the wall as you paint.

"I've recently cleared out my garage, but the floor is in a sorry state. What can I use to smarten it up?"

Use two coats of concrete floor paint, but be sure to wash the floor first with a strong detergent to remove any oil or grease.

"Can I use gloss on a wooden floor?"

Yes, you can, but it won't be as hardwearing as specifically prepared floor paint.

"The reveals around my windows keep going green, are covered with black spores and are difficult to keep clean. They are painted with a water-based acrylic. Any ideas?"

Wash with bleach, rinse it well, and paint with an oil-based paint, which is more hardwearing and easier to wipe.

"I want to strip my doors but fear that it's a lot of work. Are there other options?"

Yes, use a wood-graining kit to create the appearance of real wood. It's also much greener than using all the chemicals required to strip back lots of coats of old paint.

"We've recently moved to an old house and have just cleaned up the old oak beams. What should we treat them with?"

Give them a single coat of matt varnish and they will look like they have been beautifully waxed.

"I've got an old exposed brick wall in my house that I'd like to keep, but it is very dusty. What can I treat it with?"

Vacuum the entire wall and apply a solution of 1 part PVA to 5 parts water to bind the surface.

"How do I varnish my newly sanded floor?"

Vacuum the floor well, and wipe it down with a damp sponge before applying the first coat. Allow it to dry and give it a light sand with fine grade paper. Then vacuum, wipe down and apply another coat of varnish.

"My floor varnish seems to yellow with age. Why?"

It must be an oil-based product. Use a water-based varnish next time. It's less smelly and dries quickly, so you can apply at least two coats in a day.

"What's the quickest way to smarten up an old wooden floor?"

Give it two coats of floor paint.

"I'm painting some stencil patterns in my child's bedroom, but the paint keeps running. How can I stop this?"

Don't put so much paint on the stencil brush. It must be almost dry.

"Why do my stencil designs look so flat and boring?"

Add depth by shading around the edges of the design. This will give the illusion of 3-D.

"I keep smudging my stencil patterns. Is there something wrong with my technique?"

Make sure the stencil is secured with low-tack masking tape when working on it, and lift it rather than slide it off the wall when you move it.

"I want to do a sponged paint effect. Can I use any old sponge?"

No, it has to be a natural sea sponge, as it won't work with a synthetic one.

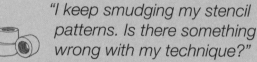

"Can I paint the underside of my cast iron bath?"

Yes, give it two coats of eggshell.

"How do I clean paint off electrical sockets?"

Use a window scraper, then polish with a cloth.

"When I store paint in my garage, it always goes hard or has a thick skin when I open it again. What can I do?"

After using paint, make sure the tin is securely closed, turn the tin upside down and back up again. This creates an airtight seal.

"How do I clean my paint brushes?"

If you are using water-based paint, wash them thoroughly with soapy water, rinse and shake dry. With oil-based paints, wash the brushes in white spirit, then soapy water, rinse, and shake dry.

"I can never remember which paints I've used where. Is there an easy system?"

Yes, label cans with the room they were used in and the date, which is always useful to know.

"How do I store my paint brushes?"

Once clean, wrap them in brown paper, and secure with a rubber band to hold the bristles together to stop them going out of shape.

"I want to have the lower half of my wall papered and the upper half painted. How do I make the join?"

Making a perfectly level cut in the wallpaper is tricky, so disguise the join with a paper border or dado rail.

"I want to wallpaper my living room. Where do I start?"

Close to a corner or above a door so that if the pattern doesn't quite match, it will be less noticeable.

"What is a pattern repeat?"

It's the size of the pattern on wallpaper from its exact beginning to its exact end (vertically). Patterns with large repeats produce more wastage than smaller pattern repeats when the paper is hung and adjoining strips are trimmed to get an accurate pattern match.

"How do I get the first length of wallpaper straight?"

Use a spirit level to draw a vertical pencil line on the wall.

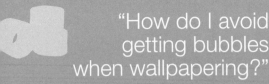

"How do I avoid getting bubbles when wallpapering?"

Firstly, allow the wallpaper to soak for a few minutes after it has been pasted, before you hang it on the wall. Secondly, smooth the paper to remove any bubbles as you are hanging it.

"How do I fold my wallpaper while it soaks, without creasing it?"

As you paste it, keep folding it back on itself to form a loose concertina, where only pasted surfaces touch each other.

"I've got lots of wallpaper lengths pasted; how do I keep track of which one should be next?"

When you leave one to soak, write on the back what time it will be ready.

"How do I get rid of my woodchip wallpaper?"

Score it first with the edge of a scraper to break up the surface (this also works for vinyl papers) and then use a steam stripper. It's a slow job but satisfying when it's done.

"I've wallpapered my dining room but in places there seems to be bits of grit trapped behind the surface. How can I get rid of them?"

Very gently, use a hammer to tap the grit flat.

"Is expensive wallpaper easier to hang than the cheaper versions?"

Generally, the cheaper stuff is the easiest to hang. Think about hiring a professional for the pricy prints.

"We've taken out a fitted wardrobe and need to patch in the wallpaper. We've got some spare in the attic. Can I use it?"

Yes, if the paper on the walls has not faded. Try to strip the existing paper back to a full-width strip so you have a straight edge to work with.

"My friend told me that you can't use wallpaper in a bathroom. Is this true?"

Condensation is certainly an issue for paper in bathrooms, but as long as it is well ventilated and you use a vinyl paper, you should be ok.

"I can see white joins along my wallpaper edges. What can I do?"

Use a felt tip pen to match the background of the paper, and carefully draw down the joints to disguise them.

"Why do I get shiny seams and patches on my wallpaper?"

It's paste on the surface. Be sure to remove paste before it dries using a clean damp sponge.

"I always seem to get paste on the front of the wallpaper. Any tips?"

After you've pasted a length, always wipe down your pasting table with clean water.

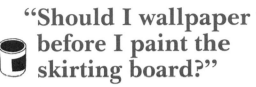

"Should I wallpaper before I paint the skirting board?"

No, always do the painting first and overlap the paint onto the wall, then paper on top.

"I've snagged my wallpaper and made a small tear. How can I repair it?"

Simply apply a little PVA or border adhesive to the wall and carefully smooth the paper back in place with a damp sponge.

"Should I take any notice of the batch numbers on wallpaper?"

Make sure they're all the same, as slight variations can occur between batches.

"How can I protect my wallpaper from dirty marks?"

If it has a vinyl surface, it should wipe down easily. If not, apply a coat of matt varnish. Do a test patch first, just to check it doesn't damage the paper.

"I want to hang wallpaper on just one wall. How do I get a good fit in the corners?"

Draw a vertical pencil line on the wall using a spirit level, at a distance from the corner that is slightly less than the width of paper you are using. Hang a length of paper butting up to the line on the side furthest from the corner, then hang the piece on the corner side of the line, trimming the edge to fit neatly into the corner.

"Why does my wallpaper paste go all lumpy when I mix it?"

Probably because you put all the powder into the water at once. Sprinkle slowly and keep stirring all the time to make sure the powder disperses evenly.

"I'm thinking of wallpapering my bedroom but I always get paste everywhere. Is there an easy way?"

Try using ready-pasted paper: it's a lot cleaner to use!

"When I trim my wallpaper with scissors, I find it difficult to keep a straight line. What else can I try?"

Some people find it easier to trim using a craft knife, but make sure you've got a good stock of new blades as they blunt quickly.

"Why does the pattern on adjacent strips of wallpaper match at the top of the design but not the bottom?"

Wallpaper can stretch when pasted and applied, and so always make sure your pattern matches at eye level where it is most noticeable.

"My friend told me that I must line the walls with lining paper before wallpapering. Is this true?"

Strictly speaking, yes, this will provide the best finish. But if the walls are in good condition, wallpaper away without lining first.

"How do I ensure lining paper stays well stuck down around the edges?"

Smooth caulk round all joints, especially by the skirting board and in corners.

"I want to hang a border on my wallpaper. How do I keep it level?"

Use a spirit level and pencil to draw a line on the paper, and overlap the very edge of the border over this line as you smooth it into place.

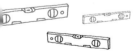

"I want to use a border as a frame to the wall. What do I do at the corners?"

Overlap the lengths and use a craft knife to cut a diagonal line through the two overlapping pieces into the corner. Peel back to remove the excess and smooth down.

"How do I wallpaper around wall-mounted lights?"

Turn off the power supply at the consumer unit or fuse box, take the lights off the wall and wrap insulating tape around the separate wires. Paper the wall and pull the wires through a small cut in the paper. Once dry, replace the lights.

"Can I wallpaper over old wallpaper?"

Yes, if the old paper is well stuck down. This can be an expensive gamble as you won't know for sure until the new wallpaper has dried!

"Why do the joins keep lifting when I am hanging wallpaper?"

Because it is the edge of the paper, it always dries out quickest. You need to reapply some paste under the edges, smooth them back in place and sponge clean. You can also use a seam roller to help keep the joins flat.

"I keep tearing my wallpaper when I try to slide it into position. It's driving me mad, what can I do?"

Always size the walls before wallpapering: apply a very dilute wallpaper paste mixture to all the walls and allow it to dry. This provides a less porous surface over which the newly pasted paper can glide.

"Do you always hang lining paper horizontally?"

No, not necessarily. It's best to hang the paper to create the fewest number of joins. For narrow walls go vertically, for wide walls go horizontally.

"I've heard that some people double-line their walls. Why would you do this?"

Simply to make it even smoother.

"I want to refit an existing shelf after wallpapering. What's the best way to mark the fixing holes?"

Remove the shelf, but refit the screws. These will protrude through the paper when you hang it and therefore mark the right positions.

"How can I get marks off wallpaper?"

Try using a pencil eraser, but be gentle.

"*What can I do with leftover wallpaper?*"

It's perfect for lining drawers.

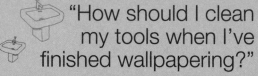

"How should I clean my tools when I've finished wallpapering?"

Use hot soapy water and make sure that they are rinsed thoroughly.

"How do I remove old tile adhesive?"

Use a wallpaper steam stripper. It softens it up and then it can be scraped off easily.

"Do I have to remove old tiles before re-tiling?"

No, not if the existing ones are firmly stuck down. Just make sure they're clean and tile straight on top as normal. However, allow longer than normal for the adhesive to dry before you grout them.

"I'm tiling on top of old tiles but the odd one is loose. Do I need to take them all off?"

No, just remove the loose ones and fill the hole flush with some exterior grade filler.

"Can I tile over shiny painted surfaces?"

Yes, but score the surface first.

"Can I tile on painted walls?"

Yes, as long as the paint is not flaky.
If it is, sand it flat and seal the surface
with a solution of 1 part **PVA** to
5 parts water.

"There are lots of switches in my kitchen. How do I tile around them neatly?"

*Turn off the power, loosen the screws in the switch
face plates and cut the tiles so that they fit behind
the switch edges by about 10 mm (⅜ in). You may
need longer screws when you re-fix the switches.*

"How can I cut a right angle section out of a tile?"

You'll need an electric tile cutter, which has a rotating cutting wheel. Standard score-and-snap tile cutters are great, but can only cut across the entire width of a tile, not smaller distances. Electric tile cutters can be hired.

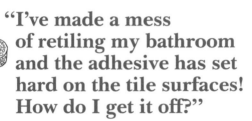

"I've made a mess of retiling my bathroom and the adhesive has set hard on the tile surfaces! How do I get it off?"

A sponge and warm water will soften it, then use a window scraper for stubborn bits. Be careful not to scratch the tile surfaces.

"My tiles keep slipping down the wall before the adhesive has dried. How do I stop this?"

On large areas, temporarily nail a wooden batten to the wall to support the first (and second lowest) course of tiles, using a spirit level to position it. When the tile adhesive has dried, remove the batten and lay the bottom course of tiles.

"My grout looks dirty. How do I smarten it up?"

There are two options: 1. Remove the old stuff with a grout rake and then re-grout. 2. Apply grout reviver: you just paint it on and wipe it off the tiles.

"How can I get a professional grout finish?"

Use a special grout shaper to smooth the joints.

"I've just retiled my new shower. How do I keep the grout white and clean?"

Paint on grout protector and wipe off the excess.

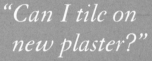

"Can I tile on new plaster?"

Yes, but prime it first with a solution of 1 part PVA to 5 parts water. This stops the adhesive drying too quickly.

"How can I revamp my old tiles without replacing them?"

Clean them thoroughly and apply two coats of tile paint.

"How can I brighten up plain white tiles?"

Use tile transfers: they're quick and easy.

"I've got some handmade tiles for my bathroom but there seems to be different shades. Will this matter?"

Randomly shuffle all the tiles to even out any difference across the finished surface.

"Why do some tiles have glazed edges?"

They are designed for placing in exposed external corners.

"I'm using large marble tiles and want to keep the joins tight. What spacers should I use?"

Thin card is ideal.

"How do I keep neat joins on external corners?"

Use an electric tile cutter to create 45° joins.

"How do I cover the cut edges of tiles on an external corner?"

Use a plastic edging strip.

"Can I tile over wallpaper?"

No. But you can fix tiles so that their edges overlap the wallpaper edge to prevent the paper edge lifting.

"I'm tiling my bathroom. How do I know how many tiles I need?"

Measure the area you want to tile (width x height = area). Take this to the tile shop and they'll work out how many tiles you need of your chosen design. Buy a few extra in case of breakages.

"I've seen some really cool glass tiles, but they're expensive. How can I incorporate them in my design?"

Use them as a border running straight through the main design.

"I'm tiling over a dark wall with glass tiles. Will their be show through?"

Probably yes, so it's best to paint the area white first.

"Do you need to seal tiles before you stick them on the wall?"

No. But if the tiles are unglazed, seal them before you grout to stop the grout staining their surface.

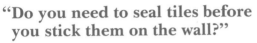

"Do I have to remove tile spacers before I grout?"

Yes, if they're thin tiles as the spacers will show through the grout. No, if they are chunkier tiles.

"I want to tile around a big pipe in my bathroom. How do I know where to cut the tiles?"

Cut a paper template to the same profile as the pipe, and stick it on a tile to provide a guideline.

"How do I cut a curve in a tile?"

Using a tile saw. It's like a hacksaw but with a round rasp-like blade.

"How do I cut a hole in a tile?"

With a tile hole cutter attachment on an electric drill.

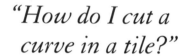

"I've bought some rustic tiles for my kitchen. How can I use tile spacers with them if the edges are so uneven?"

You can't, so use a quick-drying adhesive and, if necessary, some card to keep joins as consistent as possible.

"Can I tile over floorboards?"

Yes, but first make sure they are fixed down securely. Fix sheets of 10 mm (⅜ in) plyboard over the top and you're ready to tile. Make sure you use flexible adhesive and flexible grout.

"I'm tiling my wet room. Are all grouts the same?"

No. Some are more waterproof than others. Make sure you get a completely waterproof grout from your supplier.

"I want to tile my kitchen worktop, but I'm worried that normal grout will stain too easily. What should I do?"

Use epoxy grout. It's very hardwearing and hygienic.

"I've heard epoxy grout is hard to use. Is this true?"

It is tricky stuff. As soon as you have filled the joins, carefully rub the tiles with a wet kitchen scourer (non-scratch) to clean the tile surfaces and smooth the grout.

"I want to use mosaic tiles in my bathroom. Do I have to use a spacer between each tile?"

No. Mosaic tiles come grouped together on backing sheets, making it easy to apply large numbers in one go.

"Is grout always white?"

No, you can buy powders to mix with the grout to produce any shade you like.

"I'm about to tile around my new bath. How do I ensure no leaks?"

Run a bead of silicone around the edge of the bath where it meets the wall, and allow it to dry before you start tiling. Silicone the join again after tiling and grouting. This produces a good double seal.

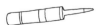

"Do I put the tile adhesive on the wall or the tile?"

Professionals put it on the wall first with a notched spreader and then apply the tiles. However, you can put adhesive on the tiles, one at a time, and fix them to the wall. This is slower, but easier for the beginner.

"My concrete floor is very bumpy. Can I tile straight on top of this?"

You can, but it's easier to use a self-levelling compound to fill in the depressions in an old concrete floor before you tile.

"Why does my tile adhesive go all lumpy?"

If you've mixed it yourself, it may be drying before you get it on the wall, so mix it in smaller batches next time. If it's a ready-mixed product, keep the lid on the tub when you're not using it.

"I'm confused: should I tile a shower before I fit the screen, or fit the screen first?"

Tile first, fit the screen later.

"How do I tile a border around a splash back using long thin border tiles?"

Cut the border tiles 45° at the corners to create a right-angle join, or use square insert tiles.

"When I cut my tiles, the edges are sometimes rough. How can I smooth them?"

Use a tile file.

"My pencil won't mark a tile when I'm measuring for a cut. What can I do?"

Use a waterproof felt tip pen instead.

"How do you tile around a shower rail without removing it?"

You don't! Take it down, do the tiling and re-fix the rail. It's easy to drill holes in tiles using a tile drill bit.

"Can I tile my bath panel?"

Yes, if it's rigid, but make sure you can remove it to gain access underneath the bath.

"What can I do with leftover tile pieces?"

Use them for mosaics or put them in the bottom of flower pots for drainage.

"I want to do a brick bond tiling pattern, but the spacers don't fit. What should I do?"

Snap off one arm of each spacer, making them into T-shapes.

"I want to tile around a column. What tiles should I choose?"

As small as possible, therefore mosaic tiles would be ideal.

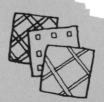

notes

Finishing touches

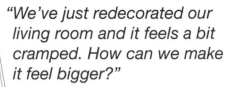

"We've just redecorated our living room and it feels a bit cramped. How can we make it feel bigger?"

Put a large mirror on one wall to reflect light and give the impression of space.

"How can I disguise the screw heads in the mirror I've just fixed to the wall in my living room?"

Use mirror screws. These have a decorative domed cap that fits on to the head of the screw.

"I want to fix some mirrors to the panels in my door. What is the best way of doing this?"

Simply use mirror grab adhesive on the back of the mirror and carefully press it in place.

"I have a very heavy ornate mirror, and I'm worried that the fixings won't be strong enough. How can I solve this problem?"

Fix a batten to the wall under the bottom edge of the mirror. Paint the batten to match the wall.

"I've seen some self-adhesive mirror pads. Are these really ok to use?"

With small mirrors, yes.

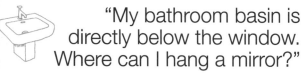

"My bathroom basin is directly below the window. Where can I hang a mirror?"

The best option is buy a mirror with a telescopic arm. Fix it on the wall to the side of the window and pull it across over the basin when you need it.

"How do I hang a row of pictures level on the wall?"

The secret is to measure the distance from the picture wire when pulled taut to the top edge of each picture. Use a spirit level to draw a horizontal guideline on the wall in pencil where you want the fixings to be, then arrange the fixings along the line, spacing them evenly.

"I want to hang some pictures on the wall down the stairs, but am worried that the children will knock them off as they run up and down. Is there an alternative to picture wires?"

Yes, simply use plate fixings, which screw to the picture frame. Screws are inserted through the plates into the wall.

"When I nail a picture hook into the wall, how can I stop the surface crumbling?"

Put some masking tape over the spot where the nail is going in. This helps bind the surface together.

"What is the best height to hang pictures?"

Ideally so the middle of the picture is at eye level.

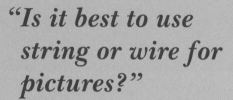

"Is it best to use string or wire for pictures?"

It's best to use wire, as string will stretch or even break over time.

"How do I tighten picture wire?"

Thread the wire through the eye at either end of the picture, then bring the two ends back to meet in the middle, making a double-thickness of wire. Use pliers to twist the two ends together, which will gradually make it tauter.

"How can I make my pictures really stand out on the wall?"

Add an extra frame using some painted door architrave. This can be attached to the wall with double-sided tape.

"How can I screw a hook into a brick wall?"

The same way you insert a screw. Drill a hole with a masonry bit and push in a plastic wall plug before screwing in the hook.

"I'm trying to hang a heavy picture on a hollow wall and I haven't got a stud detector. Is there another way to find a timber stud?"

Tap along the wall surface until the hollow sound deadens. This normally indicates stud position.

"I need a cheap picture solution. Any ideas?"

Use all your holiday snaps to make a collage in a simple picture frame.

"We've finished decorating and can't decide where to hang our pictures. Any advice?"

Hang smaller pictures in groups: three or five is ideal. Centralize larger pictures on the walls, or position them over furniture.

"How can I breathe new life into an antique picture frame?"

Ornate frames can be re-gilded using Dutch metal. Size is applied to the frame surface and wafer-thin sheets of gold metal are laid onto the frame and dabbed into the profiles using a soft paint brush.

"What's the best way of hanging a huge poster on a wall?"

Stick it up using wallpaper paste.

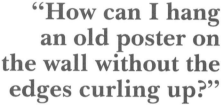

"How can I hang an old poster on the wall without the edges curling up?"

First, use a cool iron to smooth it flat, then mount it on thin card using spray mount adhesive.

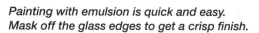

"How can I update my old picture frames to match our new decor?"

Painting with emulsion is quick and easy. Mask off the glass edges to get a crisp finish.

"Have you any ideas on trying to co-ordinate curtains, cushions and rugs?"

Simple schemes tend to bring a more harmonious feel to a room; too many different features will often lead to a very cluttered look.

"Our bathroom has finally been finished but whenever I have a shower, the bathroom mirror mists up. What can we do?"

You could change the mirror for a heated one that won't steam up.

"How can I hang a rug on the wall?"

Nail a carpet gripper rod to the wall and attach the end of the rug to it.

"What's the best way to hang a silk rug on the wall?"

Screw two cup hooks to the wall. Thread a length of wooden dowel through the looped tassels of the rug, and rest the dowel on the hooks.

"The pipework under my bathroom basin is so unsightly. Is there a quick and cheap way of disguising it?"

Fix a length of self-adhesive Velcro around the edge of the basin. Fix the other side of the Velcro to a curtain cut to size. Press the curtain in place to hide the pipe work and provide a more decorative finish.

"I want to fix a soap dish to my tiled shower wall, but I'm worried I'll crack the tiles. Any advice?"

If you choose your soap dish carefully, you should be able to find one with the screws arranged horizontally so you can make the holes in a gap between the tiles. If not, drill the holes with a tile drill bit on a slow speed.

"The cord pull in my bathroom is very dirty. Are they easy to change?"

Yes, look at the top and you should find a small acorn shape that you can unscrew and replace with a new one. The new one doesn't need to be a cheap white plastic one!

"Can I change the flush handle on my toilet?"

Yes, but investigate inside the cistern to see what will be compatible with the existing inlet valve.

"When I drill into tiles, the fine dust seems to stain the grout and sealant between my tiles. How can I avoid this?"

Hold a vacuum cleaner nozzle under the hole as you drill into the wall.

"How can we give our new bathroom a final lift?"

It's very simple to fit a new toilet seat. There are lots of exciting colours and designs these days. You can even buy non-slamming ones!

"I have sloping roof windows, so how on earth do I fit curtains?"

These windows can be fitted with blinds. Simply contact the a blind manufacturer with your window size and they'll supply all you need.

"Can I fit a new Venetian blind to existing fittings on a window?"

No, but the good news is that the vast majority of new blinds are supplied with new brackets and good instructions.

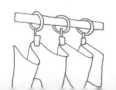

"Can I revive old Venetian blinds?"

You can give them a good clean and paint them using aerosol spray paint.

"I need to put curtains up but the walls are papered. Is it possible to attach curtain poles without damaging the wallpaper?"

Yes, but it depends on your walls and the size and weight of the curtains and pole. For stud walls you'll need hollow wall plugs to secure the fixings. For solid masonry walls, be sure to use a masonry bit in your drill and use wall plugs to get a secure fixing.

"How can I make curtain poles bend round the shape of my bay window?"

Plastic tracks will bend easily, and there are metal poles with grooved sections in parts of the pipe that allow you to bend the pole as required. Wooden poles will have to be custom made.

"How do I join curtain poles as I have a large living room window?"

Wooden poles are easy to join using a dowel screw, which literally screws into the two ends of the poles.

"What's the best way to curtain a dormer window?"

It's always a problem, but roller blinds will be the least obtrusive.

"We've redecorated on a budget. How can I update my curtain dressings?"

Keep the same curtain poles but choose some new finials with an exciting design.

"Are there any alternatives to curtain poles and tracks?"

Use thick wire suspended between two cup hooks. The curtains will need eyelets so the wire can thread through them to support the curtains.

"We've got lots of windows and need a cheap curtain solution. Help!"

Use lining fabric for the curtains themselves, and stamp your own designs on them with fabric paint.

"My son's bedroom curtains are too thin and let in the light. Will lining them make a big difference?"

Yes, but a simpler solution is to buy a black-out blind to hang behind the curtains.

"How can I get more light into a small bedroom with a single window?"

Fix made-to-measure mirrors on both window reveals to reflect more natural light into the room.

"I need to revive some old curtains. Any ideas?"

Attach some new braid or trim around the edges, or, depending on the type of fabric, you could dye them. You can have this done professionally if the lengths are too long to hand in your washing machine.

"How can I stop my curtains snagging on the pole?"

Add more curtain rings, or use a silicone spray to lubricate the pole.

"Can I paint curtain poles?"

Yes, use an aerosol and then it's much easier to do the rings as well.

"I love my curtains but how can I create a new look?"

Cut them down in size to create café-style curtains, which cover just half the height of the windows.

"Our ceilings are very low. Can I hang curtains from brackets fixed to the ceiling?"

Yes, but make sure the fixings go into wooden joists in the ceiling to take the weight of the curtains.

"I've bought a roller blind but it is too wide. Can I cut it down?"

Yes, but you'll need a hacksaw if the roller is metal. Use scissors to cut the blind material.

"Can I paint a plain roller blind?"

Yes, use fabric paint. Why not use stencils to create a simple design?

"How can I revive curtains that have been faded by the sun?"

Transform them with a fabric dye.

"What are my choices if I don't want to see curtain tracks or poles?"

Pelmets are the main option. They can be painted or covered in fabric.

"What's the best way to fix a valance to a pelmet?"

Use Velcro so that it can be removed for cleaning.

"How long should curtain poles be in relation to the window?"

For small windows, they should extend 15 cm (6 in) past the window at each end. For larger windows, this distance may double to allow the curtain to be drawn right back past the window.

"How can I change the dynamics of a square room?"

Go for round options when you choose rugs and cushions.

"How can I soften the look of my bed?"

Fix a hook in a joist above the centre of the bed head and knot some fabric on the hook, draping it back to the bed head on either side.

"How do I drill into a melamine shelf for mug hooks?"

Use a wood or hss (high speed steel) bit to drill pilot holes. Both will cope with melamine just fine. The little point on the end of a wood bit makes it the easier of the two to use in this situation.

"Help. I recently bought an illusion shelf but I have no idea how to put it up!"

First go back to the shop, as the shelf should come with a bracket system. Otherwise, if it's wood, you'll have to drill holes in the back of the shelf edge, and corresponding holes in the wall. Lengths of threaded bolt can be inserted into the shelf edge and wall respectively. Resin (strong adhesive) can be used in the holes to secure the bolts in place.

"How can I protect my kitchen shelves from wear and tear?"

Self-adhesive vinyl coverings can be stuck to the tops of the shelves to make them easy to wipe down.

"What's the simplest way of fitting a shelf in an alcove?"

Draw a line at shelf height on the side walls and back wall of the alcove, using a spirit level. Fix wooden battens at this height. Cut a sheet of MDF to the required dimensions to make the shelf. Fix it in place on the battens with panel pins or wire nails.

"How long should the screws be if I'm fixing a length of batten to the wall?"

The screws should be three times the depth of the batten.

"We've gone for a modern look but our wooden alcove shelves look a bit old fashioned. Can we try something else?"

Change them for toughened glass shelves.

"I'm hanging some shelves and am trying to mark the wall through the brackets to show where I need to drill holes. The problem is my pencil won't fit through the hole. What can I do?"

Use the point of a bradawl to make a small indent in the wall instead.

"Our dresser needs revamping now the kitchen is finished. Any thoughts?"

If it has glass doors, you can create interest by applying wallpaper or paint to the insides of the cupboards.

"How can I make the square front edge of my MDF shelving look more decorative?"

Use a router with a rounded cutter to make a smooth, rounded edge. If you're not confident with a router, use panel pins to tack some half-round moulding to the front edge of the shelf.

"How can I make best use of a storage shelf in my garage?"

Screw jam jar lids to the underside of the shelf. The jars can then be tightened on to the lids, making an ideal storage system for nails and screws.

"I've got a very small kitchen. How can I create more storage space?"

Fix open shelves across the window reveal. Use the space to store glasses so you don't lose too much light.

"There's not enough room in my kitchen to store all my pots and pans. Any tips?"

Fix a hanging rack to the ceiling for suspended storage of pots and pans. This should free up more cupboard space.

"I need more room for food preparation. Any ideas?"

Fix some substantial open shelving on the walls to get large items off the worktops, such as toasters and food processors, for example.

"How can I create more worktop space?"

Fit a hinged section of worktop that can go over your sink.

"Must I use those plastic channels that have been supplied with my kitchen plinth boards?"

Yes, they must be clipped on the bottom edge of the plinth to protect it from water penetration when you mop the floor.

"Is there a good use for leftover wooden worktop?"

Cut it down to make a bread board.

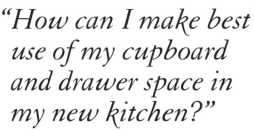

"How can I make best use of my cupboard and drawer space in my new kitchen?"

Buy some custom-made dividers to separate areas within units to make storage more organized.

"We have a new laminate worktop and have ironed on the edging strips at the ends, but however carefully you trim, you still get little white edges on the corners where you've had to cut the strip to fit. What can we do?"

Use an indelible felt tip pen to match the worktop, and run it along any white bits.

"I've just scorched my new worktop and I can't afford to replace it. Help!"

Why not integrate a food preparation panel into the area? There are some attractive stainless steel panels, for example, that would do the job.

"What's the best way to create a recycling area in my new kitchen?"

There are now many recycling bin kits available that fit into standard units.

"We're using our old fridge in our new kitchen but the door now opens the wrong way. Can we change it?"

In most cases, yes. Investigate below the seals around the edge to see if there are any predrilled holes that suggest you can move the hinges and handle.

"My new wood-effect plinth looks nothing like wood. What are my options?"

Because it's a relatively small area, it won't cost you much to buy some real wood for the plinth and stain it to match the units.

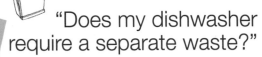

"Does my dishwasher require a separate waste?"

No, it can be directed into the U-bend below the kitchen sink using an easily fitted adaptor.

"We've fitted a big stainless steel extractor fan that doesn't vent to the outside. If it doesn't vent outside, how does it work?"

It uses charcoal filters fitted inside the hood. These will need changing from time to time.

"What's the last job I should do when finishing off a fitted kitchen?"

Make sure you have registered or sent off any paperwork regarding the guarantees on your new appliances.

"Our kitchen is finished, but we've just realized one pendant light fitting is not enough! What can we do?"

For the sake of simply swapping one fitting for another, you can change the pendant for adjustable spotlights on a bar, giving you more light where you need it.

"When we entertain in our kitchen/diner, how can I create a more intimate atmosphere?"

Fit a pull-down light that can be lowered to illuminate just the table area.

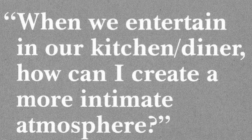

"We need to buy some new appliances for our kitchen. What should we look out for?"

Choose something with good energy efficiency: all the appliances should be labelled.

"We've changed all our kitchen units, but how can I accommodate my old fridge without it looking out of place?"

Buy some fridge paint. Clean and prepare the surface with the specified primer before applying the paint.

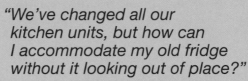

"We've totally refitted our kitchen and I think we've put in far too many low-voltage down lighters. It's way too bright."

Check the bulb size, as you may be able to change them for a much lower wattage.

"Help! I can't find where I'm supposed to attach the hot water hose to my dishwasher."

Don't panic, you probably don't need one. Most dishwashers only require a cold water supply

"There's not much room in my hallway to hang coats. Is there a space-saving option?"

A peg rail is the most unobtrusive, and you could combine it with a shelf above the rail for a little extra storage.

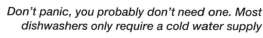

"I'm trying to fix a hanging rail in an alcove but the fixings are small and just make the wall surface crumble. Is there another way?"

It would be better to fix two much larger wooden blocks to the wall surface where you want the brackets (using screws, wall plugs and grab adhesive) and then screw the rail brackets to the blocks.

"How can I hang a heavy mobile in my son's bedroom?"

You need to find a wooden joist above the ceiling to ensure a good fixing. Either use a joist detector, or make small holes with a bradawl in the ceiling to find a joist. Screwing a hook into the joist will provide a very strong fixing for a mobile.

"I've wallpapered my bedroom, but my fitted wardrobe just doesn't look fitted any more. How can I bring it into the scheme?"

You can wallpaper the panels in the wardrobe doors if the design allows.

"How do we fix a giant plasma TV to the wall?"

If it hasn't come with a special bracket, you need to buy one. Choose one with an extending arm that allows you to adjust the position and fold it back against the wall when you need more space. Take notice of the fixing requirements for the bracket as these televisions are very heavy.

"I'm hanging a TV on the wall and want to bury the wires inside the wall. What is the best way to do this?"

It's best not to bury them. Instead, fix plastic conduit on the wall and hide the wires inside.

"Is it straightforward to put in an extra phone socket?"

Yes, you can buy extension kits. However, it is not always necessary, as wireless technology means you need a phone point for the main base unit, but other phones can be used without being plugged in to the main phone line.

"I have a small bathroom and need to make some more storage space. Any ideas?"

Create two corner shelves by cutting a large floor tile in half diagonally. Support each shelf with two jointing blocks under each wall edge.

"My computer set-up needs lots of plugs. Can I use a strip adaptor?"

Yes, but make sure it is fused and has surge protection.

"Is there any way of hiding all the wires behind my computer?"

There's no miracle yet, but a cable tidy system will certainly help with this unsightly mess!

"I want to be able to dim my bedroom lights but I don't know how to fit a dimmer switch. Help!"

Buy some touch-sensitive dimmable lamps.

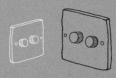

"I live in a period house and the flex on my table lamps is white and modern, which rather ruins the look. Can you offer me a solution?"

Look out for new antique-look lighting flex, which is braided and available in a variety of shades.

"The plug on the fridge is factory fitted (sealed). How can I thread this through the back of a unit?"

You can't, so cut it off, thread the wire through, and fit one that you can wire yourself.

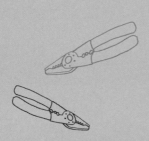

"We've just laid a laminate floor and have left a gap around the edge as instructed. It's a bit unsightly, so how do we disguise it?"

Use some quarter-round beading or Scotia moulding (wooden beading with a profile like coving). Stick it to the base of the skirting using grab adhesive. You may need one or two panel pins to hold it in place.

"I have a new wooden floor. Is there something I can use to cover the base of the pipes where they go into the floor by the radiator?"

Yes, you can buy small round pipe covers, which clip around the base of pipes to disguise any gap.

"We've ordered new carpets throughout. Is there any way we can protect them from wear and tear?"

Most manufacturers produce protective coatings that can be applied to carpets to help prevent staining and damage. Speak to your supplier, as this process is best carried out in the factory before the carpet is laid.

"How do you protect a varnished wooden floor?"

Use self-adhesive felt pads under furniture legs to prevent scratching.

"Everyone keeps tripping on the mat when they come in the front door, but we need it to protect the new carpet. Is there a compromise?"

Yes, cut out a section of carpet and underlay and replace it with a new section of coir matting. Put an appropriate threshold strip around the edge of the carpet where it joins the matting. Now you have a mat that is set in at carpet level, so no more tripping!

"How do I join two different carpets where they meet at a doorway?"

Use a threshold strip: there are many different designs, depending on the types of floor covering you are joining.

"How do I stick threshold strips down?"

They are normally nailed or screwed down.

"I have a wooden threshold strip, but don't want to screw it down as I think it would detract from the finish. Is there another option?"

Use grab adhesive and weight the strip down overnight while the adhesive dries. If you have carpet either side, be sure to trim it back to just below the lip of the strip, so the middle can stick to the floor beneath.

"Now we've decorated downstairs, all the old ironwork door handles look a bit tired. How can I spruce them up?"

Old iron door furniture can be re-blacked with matt black metal paint. Take the handles off the doors, paint them and allow to dry before fixing back in place.

"I'm painting all my black door handles, but is there any easy way of painting all the screws?"

Stick them in an old sponge so you can paint the heads without having to touch the screws.

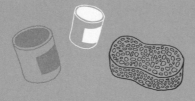

"Can I paint the glass to jazz up my windows?"

Yes, but you need glass paint. You can create a leaded-light effect by using a tube of silver outliner.

"Are there any modern equivalents to a bath mat?"

You can always use a square of hardwood duck board.

"What's a modern finish for a modern bathroom floor?"

Why not use rubber flooring? It's waterproof and warm underfoot.

"We've no space in our new bathroom for the original old radiator. What can we do?"

Replace it with a tall, thin feature radiator. There are many designs to choose from.

"I've laid a vinyl floor in my bathroom. How can I ensure it is totally waterproof?"

The only possible area for leaks is at the edges, so run a bead of silicone sealant around the edge where the vinyl meets the skirting board or wall.

"I want to put a glass shelf in my shower but I'm worried that the fixing holes I make will let in water. What can I do?"

Put a blob of silicone on the screws when you fix them in place to make a waterproof seal.

"Everything looks great in our new bathroom except for the old plastic pipe that goes out the back of the toilet. What can I do?"

Use some PVC window reviver cream to clean it up, or paint it with emulsion to match the wall.

"Our new toilet seems to rock and the plumber is not answering his phone. Is there something I can do?"

You just need some tiny wooden wedges. Fit two or three under the bottom edge of the pan, cutting them back flush with its edge. Use silicone sealant around the entire pan edge and allow it to dry before use.

"Our stained toilet bowl is detracting from our newly decorated bathroom. What is the best way to clean it?"

Scoop out the water from the bowl and pour in a strong limescale remover. Follow the manufacturer's guidelines on how long to leave it before flushing through.

"It's a bit messy where my water pipes go through the tiles into the wall. How can I smarten things up?"

Buy some pipe collars, which simply clip around the pipe and push against the wall to cover any rough edges. These can be painted to make them more unobtrusive.

"We've painted all our interior doors. How can we make them last as long as possible?"

Screw on some finger plates above the handles.

"How can I add character to a plain wooden fireplace?"

Use some ornamental wooden beading and motifs. Many are self-adhesive, and they can be painted or stained.

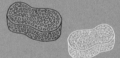

"Is there a good way of cleaning up the metal part of an old Victorian fireplace?"

Yes, you can buy metal polish for fireplaces. Wipe it on and buff it off.

"Can I change the insert tiles in my old Victorian fireplace?"

Yes, but if it's too difficult to get them out, they can always be painted.

"Our old tiled fireplace is letting down our new dining room. How can we finish it?"

Fix a new mantel shelf on top that complements the scheme in your room, then use some paint to smarten the rest up.

"We need a new coffee table for our living room but can't find one big enough. Any ideas?"

Why not buy a second-hand dining room table and cut its legs off?

"I've sanded and waxed my coffee table, but still get ring marks from glasses and cups. How can I stop this?"

Wax is not waterproof. Sand it back and varnish it.

"We're just finishing decorating our living room, but we keep arguing over how we should paint the door edge. Should it be the same as the door side in the living room?"

Yes, and the hinging edge of the door should be the same as the other side of the door.

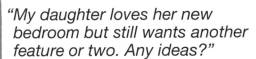

"My daughter loves her new bedroom but still wants another feature or two. Any ideas?"

How about a beaded door curtain? She could make it herself!

"What's a good way to add interest in a long hallway?"

A carpet runner along the length of the hall will certainly give it a bit of a lift.

"How can I get the best effect from my new focal point fireplace?"

Fireplaces that are just decorative can be further enhanced with interesting houseplants. Candles also give a lot of atmosphere when lit.

"Any tips on putting up flat-pack furniture?"

Make sure you have the instructions, and count all the pieces before you begin. Don't even try putting it together if you haven't got all the fixings.

"How can I make my flat-pack wardrobe a bit sturdier?"

Use glue on all the joints as you put it together.

"Is there any way to speed up putting together flat packs?"

Although most are put together with Allen keys, remember you can buy drill bits with these shapes. Always use a cordless drill/screwdriver to save time.

"I want to paint a mural on my daughter's bedroom wall. Where do I start?"

Draw a pencil grid over the design you've chosen. Scale it up onto the wall surface with some chalk and copy the picture into the squares.

"I've wallpapered my son's bedroom. Any tips on protecting the paper?"

The light switch area is most prone to dirty handprints so fit a clear plastic surround so you can wipe the area clean.

"Is there a good way to disguise a big ugly radiator?"

Putting a shelf above a radiator will certainly detract your eye from it.

"How can I stop my rugs slipping on the floor?"

Use a rubber mesh underlay to hold them in position.

"I've varnished my stair handrail, but it's a bit gritty. Can I improve the finish?"

Sand it with fine-grade paper, apply some clear wax and buff it off to give a silky smooth finish.

"My staircase is very dull and boring. How can I give it a more interesting finish?"

Add some decorative finials to the tops of the newel posts.

"How can I make the best use of an alcove for storage?"

Fit a sliding wardrobe door to enclose the whole area, and construct simple shelving inside.

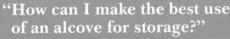

"The inside of my new fitted wardrobe is so dark. How can I get some light in there?"

If you want to avoid running wires from the mains, simply buy and fit some battery-operated strip lights, which are really simple to fit.

"What's the best way to divide off an office area in our dining room?"

Flat-pack open shelving units are quick to construct and can be secured to floor and ceiling for added stability. They also provide great storage space.

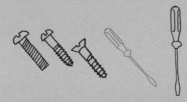

"How can I secure a fire guard around our new fireplace?"

Fix two eyelets to the walls or the edge of the fire surround and two corresponding clips to the edges of the fireguard.

"We've uncovered a fireplace. How can I test safely to see if it will draw?"

Simply use some smoke pellets.

"Is it complicated to fit an electric fire?"

Not these days, as most simply plug into a standard socket.

notes

"What's a simple way to create mood lighting?"

Fix some candle sconces on the wall and light them on special occasions.

"What type of paint should I use on a lampshade?"

Emulsion paints usually work very effectively.

"How can I change my lighting on a budget?"

Change the lampshades but keep the fittings or bases.

"We don't want to paint our copper heating pipes. How can we clean them up?"

Rub them down with wire wool and give them a coat of varnish.

"Our new oak beams seem to be splitting open. Should we be worried?"

Oak beams often split as they settle down in a new atmosphere, so this is perfectly normal.

"How can I create a drying area?"

Why not buy a clothes airer that hangs from the ceiling to keep it out of the way? Make sure the pulleys screw into joists in the ceiling.

"I've seen people put tumble dryers on top of washing machines. Is this ok?"

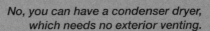

Yes, if you use a stacking kit to hold the tumble dryer securely in place. Universal kits are available.

"We've decided to have a tumble dryer. Do we need to knock a hole in the wall for ventilation?"

No, you can have a condenser dryer, which needs no exterior venting.

"My kids have just decided they need a notice board. What's a quick solution?"

If you don't want to buy a specially designed board, stick self-adhesive cork tiles on the wall.

"How can I create a notice board that matches our decor?"

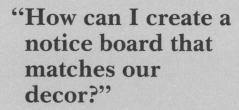

Use an offcut of curtain or sofa fabric to cover an MDF board, securing it on the back with staples. Pin ribbon in a criss-cross arrangement over the fabric, holding it in place with upholstery studs at the intersections. Photos, pictures and cards can be wedged behind the ribbons to good effect.

"Will all loft ladders fit all hatches?"

Usually yes, but measure the dimensions of your hatch and its height above the floor before buying.

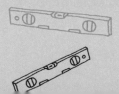

"How can I safeguard my irresplaceable family documents?"

Fit a fire and water proof chest safe.

"Where's a good place to store valuables?"

Fit a floor safe, making sure it is securely bolted to your joists.

"How can I keep my valuables out of sight?"

Fit a disguised safe, perhaps one that looks like an electrical socket.

"How can I improve the security of my front door?"

Fit hinge bolts on the hinging side and mortise door bolts on the opening edge.

"I don't want to open the door to bogus callers. What's the simplest security option?"

Buy a peep hole: they're cheap and straightforward to fit.

"Where's the best place for a key rack?"

Somewhere handy but not in direct view when the front door is open.

"Our house is finished, but we feel we need some more security devices. Is there anything we can fit at this stage?"

Wireless CCTV systems are easy to fit as they don't have to be wired into the mains supply. You can even buy solar-powered sensors.

"We love our sofa, but the fabric is very worn. What options do we have?"

The cheapest is to use a throw, or consider getting a loose cover made to give you a washable option.

"How can we provide more seating space in our small living room?"

Buy floor cushions as instant seating for visitors. Keep them to one side when not in use and they will still look decorative.

"We love our minimalist living room but want to add a bit of showy accent. Any ideas?"

Try some brightly patterned scatter cushions on your sofa.

"How can we make our doors look more modern?"

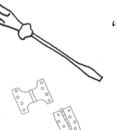

Change the hinges for polished chrome designs.

"My new sitting room has no focal point. Any simple ideas?"

Prop a tall mirror against the wall and stand a large vase of hazel branches in front of it, with a string of LED lights running through them.

"Any final tips for our authentic period living room?"

Change the electrical sockets and switches for antique-style reproductions.

"I want to smarten up my old furniture. Should I attempt a little upholstery at home?"

I wouldn't try recovering a deep-buttoned chaise longue, but recovering the seat of a simple dining chair is within most people's capability. Buy the fabric and a staple gun and give it a try.

"We've got so little space, but need extra beds when visitors come to stay. Any ideas?"

The obvious choices are inflatable beds and sofa beds. Another convenient option is a chair bed that functions in the same way as a sofa bed but takes up less room.

"It's a nightmare vacuuming under beds; there must be an easy way!"

Fit lockable casters to the bed feet.

"We live in a small apartment, and need somewhere to keep our bikes. Any suggestions?"

Manufacturers now produce all sorts of bicycle storage systems, some of which can even be hung on the ceiling, perfect for a tall hallway.

"We've finished our new nursery. Are there any safety features you recommend?"

Make sure all sockets have electrical outlet covers fixed in them.

"Our 4-year-old has just started going to the bathroom at night. How can we light his route without having all the landing lights on?"

Use a plug-in night light to provide enough illumination without waking the whole house.

"I've heard that blinds are dangerous in children's rooms. Why?"

Because of the pull cords. Make sure the cord is cut and not a continuous loop, and shorten it to be out of your child's reach.

"What's a simple way to add a final touch to our front hall?"

Hang a decorative curtain across the front door, which will not only add interest but also stop cold winter winds.

"Our old floorboards look a bit tatty now that we've redecorated. Has it got to be a replacement job?"

Try stencilling a simple border instead.

"Can I seal my old dusty flagstones?"

Yes, with a natural stone sealer as long as they have a damp-proof membrane beneath them.

"My husband wants to put down a new wood floor in our conservatory. Is this wise?"

Be careful because of the extremes of temperature. It would certainly be best to choose an engineered rather than a solid wood floor.

"Should I worry if my flagstone floor has occasional damp patches that appear on it?"

No, it sounds like there is no damp-proof membrane and they are 'breathing' naturally, so don't seal it.

"How can I revamp the old slate floor in my new kitchen?"

Clean it and give it a coat of stone enhancer.

"My toilet window is clear glass and I want more privacy. Apart from changing the window or having the curtains drawn, is there another option?"

Yes, buy some frosted film on a roll. It is self-adhesive so just cut it to size.

"How can I keep that fresh, just-finished feel to my new home?"

Move some furniture from time to time or simply move paintings and pictures round.

"How can I introduce some style into my chaotic house?"

Use lighting to give each area of your home a unique personality and make them feel separate. For example, in a kitchen/diner you need strong task lighting in the kitchen area but mood lighting in the dining area.

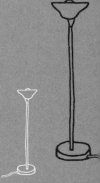

"How can I soften the look of our new kitchen/diner?"

If the lighting is sorted, why not use some tie-on cushions or even loose covers for the dining chairs?

"I'm just moving back into my newly decorated living room. I've got so much stuff, so how can I arrange it in the best way?"

This is the perfect time to be ruthless and de-clutter. Get rid of some stuff! The room will look much better for it.

"I'm doing a final clean. Can I take those grilles off the tops of the radiators to vacuum inside them?"

Yes. Carefully prise them away from the lugs with a screwdriver and lift off.

"Should I use detergents on new laminate floors?"

A simple damp (not wet) mop is the best way to keep them clean. You can also buy special wipes.

"We've redecorated, but the old carpet is letting things down. Are rugs the best option?"

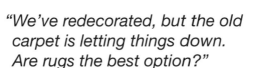

Why not just hire a carpet cleaner to breathe new life into the carpet?

"Can you clean the seals on UPVC windows?"

Most can simply be prised out, washed down with detergent, rinsed, dried and refitted.

"How can I clean up old floorboards before moving furniture back in?"

Run the edge of a filler knife or scraper down the edge of each board to remove old dirt and debris, and accentuate the board lines.

"Is it okay to give a laminate floor a coat of varnish to clean it up?"

No, varnish won't stick. Use a specially designed product called laminate floor reviver.

"How do I look after my new vinyl flooring?"

A mild detergent (washing-up liquid) solution keeps it brightest, as floor cleaners can dull the finish.

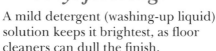

"Now we have a new water softener, do I need to keep putting salt in my dishwasher?"

Always check the manufacturer's guidelines, but if the dishwasher is now supplied with softened water, you shouldn't need salt.

"Our old gas hob is rather letting down our new kitchen as it just won't clean up. Any ideas?"

Try some stainless steel reviver, which can deal with all sorts of stains.

"What paint can I use on terracotta flower pots or bowls to match the new decor?"

Ordinary interior emulsion works fine.

"Is there a good alternative to supermarket air fresheners? I have to keep buying refills."

Bowls of aromatic dried herbs provide a very natural smell for a newly decorated room and also look good.

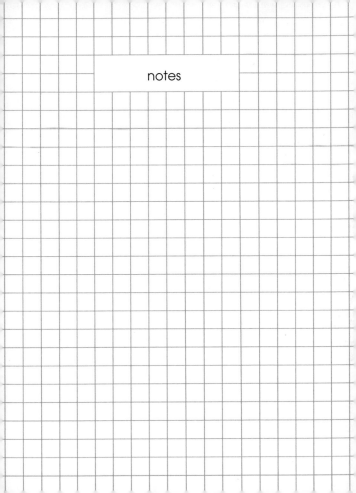

notes

Outside

"Can I paint my UPVC front door?"

Yes, but you need to choose a paint specifically designed for UPVC. Read the label, as some require a special primer.

"I want to paint my front door but I'll have to leave it open all day. Is there a way of closing it without damaging the drying paint?"

Leave it on a security chain or, if you haven't got one, fit one!

"The bottom section of my front door frame has rotted. Do I need to replace the whole thing?"

No, cut out the old wood slightly above the rot at a 45° angle through the frame. Replace the section, ensuring that the new wood has been treated with preservative, especially the end grain.

"My back door has years of paint built up on it; do I have to use a blow torch to get it all off before repainting?"

A hot air gun is much safer and easier to use. Alternatively, use a chemical stripper: there are now water-based versions which are nicer to use and not so damaging to the environment as solvent-based strippers.

"Why does my front door keep sticking?"

In wet weather, wooden doors can swell, especially if they haven't been painted along their top and bottom edges. Lift the door off, plane a little off wood if necessary, then prime and paint the edges before re-hanging it.

"Can I fit a cat flap to my UPVC back door?"

Yes, but fit it in a panel section, rather than cutting through the uprights.

"I want a front door bell. Which are the easiest to fit?"

You don't need to buy one that connects to the mains as they can be battery operated. If you're lucky, you can find a simple spring-operated model.

"My friend told me to oil my new hardwood French doors. Is this a good idea?"

Yes, if you like the natural look, but you'll have to keep doing it every year to retain the finish.

"How do I stop rain coming under my front door?"

Deflect it away by fitting a weatherboard to the bottom of the door. This is simply a shaped length of wood that can be cut to fit and fixed with four screws along the bottom edge of the door.

"Why do my garage doors keep cracking and flaking soon after I've painted them?"

Probably because they're in direct sunlight for much of the day. Try painting it a lighter colour to help reflect the heat. This will slow down the deterioration.

"Is it fine to paint a metal garage door?"

Yes. Make sure any flaky paint is sanded off and any bare metal is coated with a metal primer. After that, apply undercoat and gloss as normal.

"My garage door is one of those lightweight ones. Can I paint it?"

It's probably GRP (glass-reinforced polyester), and yes you can paint it with exterior undercoat and gloss.

"Leaves are blowing under my up-and-over garage door. What do you suggest?"

Fit a garage seal along the bottom of the door; it's like an extra-long draught excluder.

"How do I stop the rainwater seeping under my garage door?"

You need to fit a doorway drain, which must then be connected to your land drains.

"There are lots of vents on the outside of my house. Don't they let cold air in? What are they for?"

At ground level they probably let in air to ventilate under floors or provide fresh air for fuel-powered appliances. If they are higher up, they are probably fresh air intakes for appliances. **DON'T BLOCK ANY UP.**

"My brick house is so ugly. Can I paint it?"

Bricks are not really designed to be painted as they often hold moisture. However, some accept paint better than others and many people paint their brick houses successfully.

"The front of my house is so boring. How can I add some character?"

Apart from painting, have you thought about decorative window shutters, which are attractive as well as functional? You can order them online and they're easy to fit.

"I have a small garden and am worried that a fence or wall may block out light. Any ideas?"

For a short length of wall, have you considered glass blocks? They provide privacy yet still let light through.

"My flower beds touch the outside walls of my house. Will this create a damp problem?"

Not usually, as long as the soil level is below the damp-proof course.

"What do I fill the gaps around my windows with?"

Frame sealant, which comes in a tube.

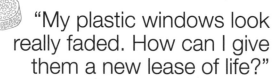

"My plastic windows look really faded. How can I give them a new lease of life?"

Easy: buy some UPVC window restorer. Clean the windows thoroughly first, wipe on the cream then buff it off.

"The sun has bleached all of my varnished window sills. How can I restore them?"

Sand them back and apply a coat of wood reviver before re-varnishing them.

"The putty around my windows is missing in places. Do I have to re-do it all?"

No, just flick out any loose bits with the end of a scraper or putty knife. Dust out the area and fill the gaps with new putty.

"There are small hairline cracks in the putty around my windows and I'm worried this is letting in water. Should I replace it?"

As long as it's stuck firm, don't replace it. Instead, mix up some filler and wipe it along the putty with the point of your finger. This fills the gaps ready for sanding and repainting.

"I'm trying to use putty but it just gets stuck all over my hands. Should I wear gloves?"

No, putty straight from the tub first needs working, a bit like bread dough! Dust your hands with some powder filler to stop it sticking to them first.

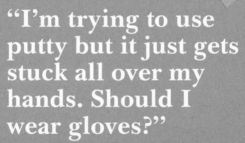

"The sun has faded my plastic gutters and downpipes. Can I paint them rather than replace the lot?"

No problem, just clean them thoroughly and apply two coats of exterior gloss.

"My windows have been treated with brown woodstain. Can I paint them?"

Yes, but give them a good sand first.

"Do I have to strip all the paint off my windows before repainting them?"

No, just remove the flaky stuff and sand them down.

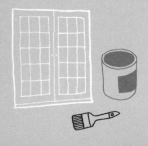

"I have an area of rot in my window sill. Is there any way to save it?"

Yes, as long as it's a contained area. First cut out the rotten wood and apply wood hardener around the hole. When dry, fill with plastic wood and sand. It's now ready to paint as normal.

"How do I stop rot returning to my window sills?"

Try preservative pellets. Simply drill holes around the rotten patch and tap the pellets in place. Fill over the top with plastic wood.

"My window sill is rotten along its whole length. Has the window got to come out?"

No, and don't waste time trying to treat it. Cut off the sill with a saw and replace it. This is probably a job for a carpenter.

"How many coats of paint should I apply to my windows?"

Prime any bare wood, then apply at least one undercoat and one coat of gloss.

"My window is broken. How do I measure for a new pane of glass?"

Remove the old pane carefully, including the putty. Measure the height and width of the frame from rebate to rebate. Subtract 2 mm (¹⁄₁₆ in) from each measurement and go to your glass supplier.

"How do I refit the wooden beading when replacing a window pane?"

Fix the lengths of beading in position by carefully nailing panel pins through them into the window rebates. Protect the glass by shielding it from the hammer edge with a piece of stiff card.

"What should I use to fill holes in my wooden windows?"

Use exterior-grade filler and be sure to use an exterior undercoat on top as it is very thick and flexible and fills small gaps.

"How do I repair rusty metal windows for painting?"

Sand them back to shiny metal and use a rust inhibitor, then a coat of metal primer. They may then be painted as normal.

"Is it safe to use a hot air gun to strip windows? I'm afraid I'll crack the glass."

Not if you use a heat shield attachment.

"How can I get rid of an old concrete path?"

Use a sledge hammer and pick axe for small paths, or hire a power breaker for large areas.

"We've moved into a new house and want to lay some paths in the garden. Where should we put them?"

Relax for a few weeks to see where you naturally walk. This gives you the blueprint for the layout.

"I have a pothole in my tarmac drive. Is this a job for the professionals?"

It doesn't need to be. Simply clean out the hole and pour in some cold-mix tarmac (buy it by the bag). Tamp it down using the end of a heavy post.

"How can I change the look of a boring concrete path around my house?"

You can lay more decorative slabs straight on top as long as you keep well below the damp-proof course.

"I want a meandering paved path but I don't want to cut lots of slabs. Is there something else I can use?"

Some manufacturers make curved slabs, or use small granite setts to create curves and corners.

"Weeds keep growing though my gravel path. How can I stop this?"

Weed killer helps, but the permanent solution is to take out the gravel, lay a weed-suppressing membrane and put the gravel back in. It's hard work, but you only need do it once!

"I have a slippery wooden walkway. Is there a way to improve grip?"

Staple chicken wire across the surface.

"I want to lay a gravel path, but what's available is boring. What else can I use?"

Try washed slate or recycled crushed glass.

"Have you got any decorative path ideas?"

Try combining two or three different materials to keep it interesting. Paving slabs combine well with areas of gravel and bricks, or try bark chips scattered around wooden stepping stones for a very attractive feature.

"How do I mark out the route for a meandering path?"

A garden hose is ideal for making curved guidelines.

"My gravel path keeps creeping on to the grass. How can I contain it?"

Dig a narrow trench along the edge of the path and use wooden pegs to secure lengths of preserved timber (often called gravel boards) in place.

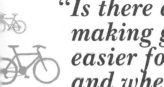

"Is there any way of making gravel paths easier for bicycles and wheelbarrows?"

Yes, you can buy honeycomb-like mats that are infilled with the gravel to make the surface much more stable.

"I'm doing some hard landscaping and need to mark out where walls and areas of paving are going. How do I make guidelines?"

String and pegs is the best way. Drizzle some sand over the string before moving it to a different place to leave a straight sand guideline.

"What's the difference between concrete and mortar?"

Basic mortar is a mixture of cement, sand and water, whereas concrete also includes larger aggregate (stones) as well.

"How do I make mortar?"

You can buy it ready mixed for small jobs (just add water). To mix your own, use 1 part Portland cement to 4 parts building sand. Mix the dry ingredients together, then add water.

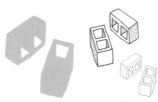

"How do I mix mortar?"

It depends how much you need. For big jobs, hire an electric or petrol-powered cement mixer. For smaller jobs, mix it in a wheelbarrow.

"My patio is very slippery. How can I make it safer?"

Use a fungicidal solution to kill algae and moss. Leave it for 24 hours before pressure washing it off. This also works on decking.

"I know I need to make sure my patio slopes away from my house, but how much should this be?"

Try to provide a fall away from the house of 1:50.

"I have a small garden and want to pave it. What type of slabs look best?"

Small areas are best done with small slabs as it makes the area look larger.

"How do I make sure my patio is square?"

You need a large builder's square. Join two lengths of wood together at right angles (just by eye) using a single nail. Measure 90 cm (3 ft) along one length and 120 cm (4 ft) along the other. At these points, attach another length of wood that is exactly 150 cm (5 ft) long. You now have a perfect 90° angle.

"Should I lay paving slabs on a solid bed of mortar or just on a few blobs?"

A few blobs uses less mortar, but a solid bed is the most secure. You can also lay slabs on a dry mix of sand and cement.

"How can I stop weeds growing through the pointing on my patio?"

Rake out the old mortar, sprinkle in some slow-release weedkiller granules, then repoint.

"I'm pointing my patio but cement keeps going all over the slabs. What am I doing wrong?"

Your mixture is probably too wet. Use a drier one and an old paint brush to remove the excess before it dries.

"Can I join a patio to the outside of my house?"

Yes, but it must be below the damp-proof course.

"I want to leave a drainage gap between the side of my house and my patio. What's the simplest solution?"

Gravel is the easiest option plus it provides good drainage.

"Why does the mortar between my patio slabs keep cracking?"

The slabs themselves are probably moving and need relaying on a firmer base.

"Do I have to use wet mortar for pointing my patio?"

No, you can brush in a dry mixture of sand and cement, then wet it with a watering can when you've finished. You can also buy ready-mixed jointing compounds.

"Can I remove cement stains from my patio?"

Use a brick acid or cleaner. It's very caustic, so remember to wear protective gloves and follow safety instructions carefully.

"My husband has laid a patio but won't finish the awkward edges. I can't cut the slabs, so what can I do?"

Why not create a decorative edge by filling in the gaps with wet mortar and pressing some pebbles or cobbles into it?

"I have some wobbly stepping stones. How can I firm them up?"

Lever them up and add a bit more sand or soil below them.

"I want to create some steps in my garden. What is the simplest option?"

Railway sleepers provide ready-made steps once they are cut to length. Stake them in position and backfill the treads if required with decorative gravel.

"A chunk of cement has broken off the front edge of my garden steps. Do I have to rebuild them totally?"

No, place a board against the front edge of the broken step, wedging it in place with a couple of bricks. Use some quick-drying mortar (you can buy it in little bags) to infill a new edge. Remove the board when it has dried.

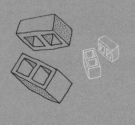

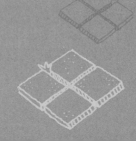

"I need loads of gravel for my garden. What's the cheapest way to buy it?"

Buy in bulk: large bags are ideal, and most companies should be able to crane it over your garden wall.

"How do I calculate how much gravel I need?"

You need to work out the area you want to cover and multiply it by the depth of gravel you want. For large quantities, give this figure to your supplier and they'll work it out. For small areas, buy around 75 kg (165 lb) of gravel per square metre (square yard).

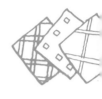

"What should I use to edge a path?"

Rows of bricks or edging tiles are good, long-lasting options. Also look out for wooden edging bundles that unravel to provide rows of wooden stakes, which are quick and easy to position.

"I've bought some decking boards, but they have a different size of ribbing on each side. Which way up should I put them?"

It's a purely personal choice; both are designed to help water run off and make them less slippery.

"I'm building a deck in my garden. What foundations do I need to make?"

You can lay decking directly on a hard level surface, such as an existing patio. Otherwise you'll need brick pillars or pressure-treated wooden posts to support the deck and make it level. The pillars will need a concrete footing and the posts will need to be concreted into the ground.

"How do I get my posts the right height for fitting my deck frame?"

When you concrete them in, leave them long. Fit the frame to the posts, then cut them flush with the top of the frame.

"What is the best way to join a deck frame to the posts? I need it to be strong."

Use two 10 mm (⅜ in) bolts at each join.

"I've bought pressure-treated boards to build my deck. Do I need to treat the newly cut ends of the decking boards with preservative as I lay them?"

Yes. If you cut a board to fit, then treat the cut end before fixing it in place.

"The ground over which I'm laying my deck is very weedy. I'm worried that the weeds will grow up through my deck. Help!"

Before you begin laying the deck, lay a weed-suppressing membrane on the ground below.

"How can I create a curved edge to my deck?"

Don't cut the edge until the deck is complete, just leave the boards longer than you require. Draw a pencil guideline to mark the curve then use a jigsaw, which will cut a perfect curve.

"Can I use any type of wood for decking? I've got some spare pine boards in the garage."

No. Always use timber that has been pressure-treated with a preservative or the boards will soon rot.

"We want a deck but there are drain covers in the way. Can we deck over the top of them?"

Yes, but make moveable panels in the deck for access.

"Do I need to leave a gap between decking boards or do I butt them tight against each other?"

You need to leave a gap to aid drainage: 2–3 mm ($\frac{1}{16}$–$\frac{1}{8}$ in) is ideal.

"What's the easiest way of maintaining a consistent gap between decking boards?"

Use some large nails as temporary spacers. Place them between the board edges as you fix them in place. The heads on the nails will stop them falling through the gaps.

"Must my decking be laid absolutely level?"

Ideally it should be laid just off level to allow water to run off the boards. If the deck is next to the house, make sure that the run off is away from the house.

"What is the best way to keep decking protected and looking smart?"

Once a year, brush it down to remove any dirt and give it a coat of decking protector.

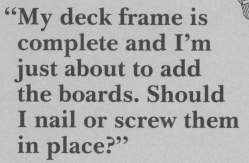

"My deck frame is complete and I'm just about to add the boards. Should I nail or screw them in place?"

Always use screws as there is less chance of the boards bowing or moving. Choose screws specially designed for decks.

"My children keep dropping things through the gaps in my deck and it's nailed down. How can I retrieve it all?"

Carefully prise up a board using a pry bar. When you've finished, screw the board back in place rather than nail it (ready for next time).

"I'm screwing down a deck but keep splitting the wood. What's going wrong?"

You need to drill pilot holes before you use the screws. Choose a wood bit that is slightly narrower than the screws you are using.

"I'm putting a new fence right the way around our garden. What's the easiest way to dig the holes for the posts?"

Hire a post auger.

"The joints in my post-and-rail fence are loose. How can I fix them?"

Tap some wooden wedges into the joints.

"How do I hold, hammer in, and position a fence post? I don't have that many hands!"

Use rubber bands to hold the spirit level on the post. This leaves your hands free for hammering it in.

"Some of the joints on my wooden gates are loosening up. Do I need to replace the gates?"

No, there are all sorts of metal-mending plates available: straight, right-angled and T-shaped, for example. These simply screw on either side of a joint to make it more secure.

"What's the best way to fix a wobbly gate post?"

If the post is rotten, replace it. If it's fine, dig a hole around the post about 30 cm (12 in) across and 30 cm (12 in) deep. Pour in a bag of post mix (ready mixed concrete designed for posts), water it in as directed on the bag and prop the post vertical until the mix dries, usually in a couple of hours.

"How do I stop fence posts leaning while the concrete sets?"

Temporarily nail a piece of batten on each side of the post. Wedge the end of each batten into the ground to hold the post secure, using a spirit level to make sure the post is vertical.

"My fence is too low but it doesn't need replacing. Can I fix more panels on top?"

No, but you could use trellis panels, which are lighter. They also provide a more decorative aspect, and you can improve your privacy by covering them with climbing plants.

"I keep splitting my fence posts when I hammer them in. What's the best way of protecting them?"

Use a specially designed post rammer, which fits over the top of the post, or hold another block of wood on top and hit this rather than the post itself.

"I need to put up a featherboard fence in a weekend. Any tips?"

You can save a lot of time by hiring a nailer to fix the boards to the frame.

"Can I use creosote to treat my fence?"

Ideally not, as there are much greener options now available. The new water-based products are also much more pleasant to use.

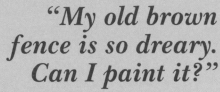

"My old brown fence is so dreary. Can I paint it?"

Yes, but it's much easier to apply a woodstain. These are now available in a whole range of exciting shades to create any mood or effect you like.

"The bottom of my boarded fence is rotten. Is there something I can do?"

Saw off the bottom 20 cm (8 in), and nail a horizontal board between the posts to cover the gap.

"Do I really have to dig holes for fence posts?

You can also use metal fence spikes, which are hammered into the ground and have a square socket in the top for the post.

"Now we've redesigned our garden, the old fence looks a bit tired and dull. What can we do to smarten it up?"

Why not use some decorative post finials? There are many different designs available.

"I'm worried about security as my garden backs on to an alleyway. How can I stop people climbing over my garden wall?"

There are various spiky strips available that fit on top of a wall. Buy them on the internet, but check with the police that they are legal first.

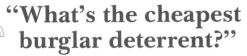

"What's the cheapest burglar deterrent?"

Fit a dummy alarm box to the front of your house.

"How can I protect my shed from burglars?"

Always make sure it has a good padlock and fit a battery-operated shed intruder alarm.

"Birds keep roosting on my upstairs window sills. What can I do?"

Anti-perch spikes are easy to cut to length and fit.

"*I want to paint the outside of my house. What paint should I use?*"

Be sure to use an exterior-grade paint. They are available in smooth or textured finishes.

"I want to paint my outside walls but am worried about the rain. How do I protect the paint while it dries?"

Check the weather forecast before you start! Most exterior paints dry quickly, however, and some are even shower-proof in just 15 minutes.

"My old rendered wall is covered in fine cracks. Any suggestions?"

Apply a textured coating to fill the cracks in. Some are coloured, so you won't need to paint the wall afterwards.

"I've seen microporous paint for sale. What is it?"

It allows moisture to dry out through the finished surface but does not allow water back the other way, making it ideal for exterior use.

"I've got trellis with climbing plants fixed to the side of my house. How can I paint the walls?"

Loosen the trellis from the wall and bring it slowly forwards to lay on the ground, plant and all. Cover with a dust sheet while paint is applied, then put it back up when finished.

"There are some cracks on the outside of my house. Should I worry about them?"

Some will be due to settlement or age, but always monitor them. Watch out for new ones or ones that keep growing.

"What should I use to fill cracks on the outside walls of my house?"

Use exterior filler for small cracks and mortar for larger ones.

"There is algae on my exterior walls. Can I paint over the top of it?"

No, apply a fungicide to kill all growth, pressure wash it off, and use paint that contains a fungicide.

"My outside walls are very old and powdery; can I paint straight on top?"

No, use a stabilizing solution first.

"I want to render the outside of my house. Should I attempt it myself?"

Filling or repairing small patches, yes. Doing the lot, no: it's a job for the professionals.

"Can I patch up Tyrolean?"

Yes, but you'll need to hire a Tyrolean gun.

"When I patch-repair render, how can I make a good join?"

When you've pressed the new render in place, allow it to dry partially (an hour or so) before going over the patch with a damp sponge in circular motions.

"Why does my render patch bulge out so much?"

You're trying to fill too deep a hole. Instead, build up the finish in two layers, allowing the first coat to dry before the next is applied.

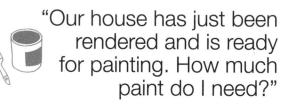

"Our house has just been rendered and is ready for painting. How much paint do I need?"

Use the can directions as a guideline. Remember that rough-cast or textured render will use at least double the amount of paint as a flat surface.

"My wall has been lime-rendered but needs some patching. Can I use ordinary mortar?"

No you should use a lime mix. Modern cement mortar is too hard and will probably crack.

"I must do some re-pointing to my brickwork. Where do I start?"

Make sure you rake out the loose material from the joints first. Press in new mortar with a pointing trowel or a brick jointer. Use a stiff brush to remove excess mortar from brick faces when it's partially dry at the end of the day.

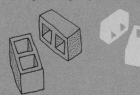

"How can I avoid wasting so much mortar when I re-point my brick garage?"

Hold a brick trowel under the joint as you work. This will act as a platform to catch any mortar that drops out of the joint.

"I suffer from graffiti on my garage wall. Any ideas?"

Use anti-graffiti paint. It is a clear product that is applied over your existing wall colour. Any graffiti can then be washed off easily with water.

"I've got a loose capping stone on my garden wall, and mortar doesn't seem to hold it in place. What will?"

The professionals wouldn't approve, but simply use some grab adhesive out of a tube and press it firmly in place: it really works!

"Can I spray paint the outside of my house?"

This is really a job for a professional.

"Can I paint my soffit board?"

Yes, but use exterior-grade emulsion.

"How can I protect my plastic windows from paint splatters when I'm painting the wall above them?"

Mask them with clear plastic dust sheets so you can still see out of them while you work.

"I want to grow some climbing plants on my house walls. Will it damage them?"

As long as the wall surface is in good condition, no.

"The bottom section of my newly painted wall gets very dirty. I've heard of dirt-proof paint; does it work?"

Not really, though some companies make claims in this area. It is better to paint a dark plinth along the bottom of the wall to disguise any dirt splashes.

"**When I paint on a sunny day, it's difficult to see what I'm doing and the paint dries too quickly, making a lumpy finish. How do I stop this?**"

It's always best to paint in the shade. Follow the sun round the house during the day.

"*What can I do to smarten up my rusty old railings?*"

Thoroughly scrub them down with a wire brush and paint with two coats of specialist rust-proof paint. If you want to spend a bit more (a lot more!), there are companies that will take them away, give them a powder coat finish and reinstall them.

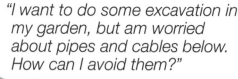

"I want to do some excavation in my garden, but am worried about pipes and cables below. How can I avoid them?"

Hire a pipe and cable detector.

"I want an outside tap to make washing the car easier. Is this a big job?"

No, you can get all-in-one outside tap kits that are easy to fit. You don't always need to turn off the water supply, but you will need to drill a hole in your wall.

"How do I stop my outside tap freezing in the winter?"

Make sure an isolation valve is fitted on the inside of the wall. In the autumn, turn off the valve, then turn on the tap outside to drain any water in the pipe and tap to stop it freezing.

"I can't reach the stopcock outside my house. Any ideas?"

Some are down narrow shafts, so you'll need to buy a stopcock key with a long handle.

"I keep slipping on my front door step. Can I cover it with something?"

Just buy some anti-slip paint and give it two coats.

"Am I allowed to have electric sockets outside?"

Yes, but they must be weatherproof outdoor sockets, with an RCD (residual current device).

"I want some lights in my garden, but am scared of installing electric cables. Do I need professional help?"

For mains-operated lights, yes, but why not try some solar-powered lights? There are no wires!

"I want my outside light to be on when I get home in the dark. Do I need to wire up a security light system?"

No, just fit a low-energy light sensor bulb in your existing outside light. It automatically comes on at dusk and goes off at dawn.

"Why does my outside security light stay on so long?"

Look for a little dial on the sensor, and set it to a shorter time.

"Why does my outside light come on during the day?"

The sensor has been set to be too sensitive. Turn it down to a darker setting.

"Why do my security light bulbs keep blowing?"

Try a lower-wattage bulb. Also, avoid touching the bulb with your fingers when installing a new one.

"Can I use low-energy bulbs outside?"

Not in security lights, but they can be used in most standard exterior fittings.

"I want to buy a water butt. Are they all the same?"

Fit one with a diverter; this stops the butt overflowing.

"My down pipe is blocked at the bottom where it disappears into the concrete path. Help!"

Cut out a 10 cm (4 in) section of pipe just above the base. Remove the blockage and rejoin the pipes with a down pipe connector.

"Can I paint my plastic garden furniture?"

Yes, clean it thoroughly first then give it two coats of gloss.

"I think my downpipes are blocked as my gutters overflow during heavy rain. How do I unblock them?"

The blockage is usually at the top or bottom, rarely the middle. Try some stiff wire, an unwound coat hanger is ideal, and simply push it in at the top or bottom of the pipe. Leave a 'hook' on the end of the wire to try to pull out the blockage (it's normally leaves).

"How do I stop my downpipes becoming blocked with leaves?"

Push a leaf guard into the top of each one.

"How do I keep my land drains from blocking?"

Make sure they have covers where necessary and keep the top grates clear of leaves and debris.

"The drain outside my kitchen window always smells: it's vile. Help!"

You need to scoop out the muck from the sump. Wearing plastic gloves, shove your hand down and pull it all out! Then flush through with drain cleaner.

"How do I lift a manhole cover? Mine seems to be jammed."

Scrape the debris out of the rim, tap round the edge with a hammer and, if it's still stuck, spray some lubricant around the edge.

"There are no handles on my manhole cover. How do I lift it?"

Some require manhole keys that can be bought from hardware shops. You'll need a pair.

"I've just laid a new patio but there's a manhole cover in the middle. What can I do to make it less ugly?"

You can buy a special cover for just this purpose. It is shaped rather like a tray, and a paving slab fits in the top to blend it in with the surrounding patio.

"How can I stop my gutters becoming blocked? They overflow when it rains."

Clear them at least once a year, removing all debris. You could also fit special mesh leaf guards that run along the length of the gutter.

"My gutter joints leak. Do I need new guttering?"

No. On a dry day, run a bead of gutter sealant around the outside of the joint to make it waterproof.

"My flat roof looks very old and I'm worried it may start leaking. Can I keep it going a bit longer?"

Yes, by cleaning it off and painting it with a waterproof acrylic roof coating.

"Puddles form on my flat roof when it rains; otherwise it appears to be in good condition. Does it need replacing?"

No, clean it down and fill in the undulations with a bitumen compound. Recoat the roof with a bitumen sealer.

"How do I repair bubbles in my flat roof?"

Cut through them with a craft knife, fill the void with bitumen sealer, flatten the flaps back and apply more sealer over the top. Finally, stick a patch of self-adhesive flashing over the top.

"I want to use some corrugated plastic for a lean-to carport, how do I cut it without it chipping?"

Sandwich it between two wooden boards held in place with clamps, which will stop it flopping about. Then cut down the edge of the wood through the sheet.

"Can I put my new garden shed straight on the lawn?"

Yes, but it will probably rot in a couple of years. It is better to support it above the ground by raising it up on concrete blocks or lengths of pressure-treated 10 x 5 cm (4 x 2 in) timber.

"What can I use to re-cover my shed roof? It is starting to peel and I'm worried it will leak."

You can use either roofing felt or shingles. Shingles can be made from felt or wood and provide a more decorative option.

"I want to build a small garden wall. Do I need foundations?"

Yes, but nothing major. For single-thickness brick walls up to 1 m (3 ft 3 in) tall, use 15 cm (6 in) of concrete. For a double-thickness wall, the concrete needs to be 25 cm (10 in) deep.

"Do I have to use poured concrete for garden wall foundations?"

If it's just a small wall, dig a shallow trench and lay a row of concrete blocks on their sides on a bed of mortar, level with the surrounding ground surface. Allow the mortar to dry, then build the wall on top of the blocks.

"How do I keep footings level if I'm building a wall on a slope?"

Step the footings rather than having a continuous depth.

"I want to build a brick arch in my garden but I'm worried it will fall down as I build it. Any ideas?"

You need to make an arch former out of wood before you begin. This will support the bricks while the mortar dries.

"I want to build my own garden wall but I'm no good at working with mortar. Are there any alternatives?"

Some walling blocks are specifically designed for this purpose and can be assembled without mortar simply using a walling adhesive.

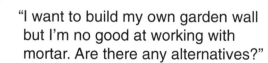

"I'm building a wall and my Mortar seems to dry too quickly on a hot sunny day. How can I slow things down?"

Dip the bricks in water before laying them.

"My new brick wall has got white fluffy powder all over it. Help!"

Don't panic, it's perfectly normal. It's called efflorescence, and forms as salts dry out through the brick surface, leaving a crystallized residue. It will disappear in time.

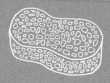

"I've got a painted retaining wall in my garden, but the paint keeps flaking off. Is there anything I can do?"

Try shovelling back the soil behind the wall, and lining the wall with a plastic membrane before backfilling. This should help reduce moisture in the wall.

"Do I need any drainage in a retaining wall?"

Yes, you must allow ground water to pass through it. Position plastic or copper pipe sections through the wall along the bottom.

"It's going to take a few weekends to complete my wall. How do I make sure that my mortar will be consistent?"

Measure exactly when mixing, using precise bucket loads of sand and cement.

"Do I need brick piers as extra support in my garden wall?"

It depends on the height of the wall. As a guide, for a single-thickness wall over 40 cm (16 in) high, build a pier every 3 m (10 ft).

"When building a wall, how do I cut a brick cleanly in half?"

Place it on a bed of sand and mark the cut all the way round with a pencil or chalk. Use a club hammer and bolster chisel to sharply tap all 4 marked sides. Keep going round until the brick breaks along the line.

"Does a wall have to have capping stones?"

No, but they do help shed water and can look decorative.

"I would like to use a yellowish mortar to match the bricks I am laying. Is this possible?"

If you fancy a change, there are additives that can be added to the mortar mix.

"I'm laying an area of block pavers. What do I need as a base?"

Lay them on a bed of compacted building sand; you don't need mortar. If you are laying a drive, you'll need a deep foundation of hardcore under the sand.

"I want to use pavers for my garden path, but I'll need to cut some for the edges. What's the easiest way?"

You can use a club hammer and bolster chisel, but it's much quicker and easier to hire a block splitter.

"What do I use to fill in the gaps between my new block pavers?"

Fine kiln-dried sand.

"The wheels of our car are making our block-paved drive uneven. How can I re-level it?"

Remove the pavers in the sunken sections using two flat-headed screwdrivers to lever them out. Infill the hollow with sand, compact it and replace the pavers. Fill the gaps between the pavers with more sand to hold them secure.

"How do I stop birds and vermin getting in my roof?"

Fit strips of wire mesh under the bottom edge of the tiles: manufacturers sometimes call these eaves filler strips.

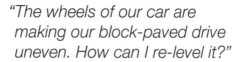

"We've recently put up a new conservatory but I'm worried that if a tile slipped off the roof it could come crashing through the glass. How can I protect the conservatory roof?"

Fix a roof tile guard, which clips around the gutter above.

"I'm tired of painting my fascia boards. Are there any alternatives?"

Yes, they can be covered with UPVC to provide a maintenance-free finish.

"It's awkward when I paint my guttering, as the top of my ladder is too close to the wall. What can I do?"

Use a ladder stand-off. This clips to the top of the ladder and brings you back off the wall surface to make jobs like painting the gutters much easier.

"When I'm painting my upstairs windows, how can I hold on to the ladder, the paint and the brush at the same time?"

Use a paint reservoir, which clips to the top of the ladder, or an S-shaped hook designed for holding a paint kettle or small can.

"I want to clad the outside of my house. What choices do I have?"

There are many choices of materials, including wood, aluminium and UPVC. You can also get cement board, which lasts for ever (well, nearly), comes ready finished and looks like beautifully painted wood.

"I need a ladder but have nowhere to store it. Any ideas?"

Look out for a telescopic ladder, which can literally shrink down smaller than a stepladder. They are expensive, however.

"How do I stop the base of my ladder slipping when I'm working on it?"

Always have someone holding the base, and place the bottom on a strong board when working off a soft surface.

"My car has dripped oil all over my tarmac drive. Help!"

Buy some oil patch cleaner, dilute it with hot water and scrub away.

"How can I brighten up my wooden garden furniture?"

Hardwoods can be cleaned, sanded and treated with oil to restore the finish. Softwoods, once cleaned and sanded, can be stained, varnished or painted.

"My lead flashing is cracked and leaking. Does it have to be replaced?"

Not always. Try applying flashing primer and some self-adhesive lead repair tape.

"I'd love to have a water feature but I'm worried about my young children: what's the safest option?"

Pebble fountains are ideal as they don't have an exposed reservoir.

"My pond is leaking, and I think it has a rubber liner. Can I fix it?"

Drain the pond and locate the hole. Ensure it is bone dry, then sand the area to give it a key. Mend it with a patch kit.

"Can I stop my garden pond going green?"

Yes, you can buy chemicals to treat the water during the summer months. Avoid a build-up of organic matter, such as leaves or uneaten fish food, in the water as this feeds the algae.

"There's a crack in my concrete-lined pond. Can I do anything about it?"

Drain the pond and enlarge the crack to make a V-shape profile. Combine some mortar with water proofer, and press it in place with a trowel. Once dry, paint it with a waterproof sealant.

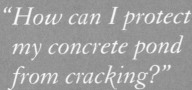

"How can I protect my concrete pond from cracking?"

During the winter months, place an old plastic ball in the water. This relieves any pressure exerted on the concrete by ice as it freezes and thaws.

"I want to make a pond in my garden. What are my options for lining the hole?"

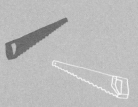

There are four main options:
1. a rubber liner,
2. a rigid plastic liner,
3. concrete blocks and waterproof render, or
4. natural clay.

"My children want a tree house. What wood should I use to build it?"

Softwood is the cheapest, but make sure it has been pressure-treated with preservative so it lasts.

"Do I need special sand for my child's sandpit?"

Yes, it must be washed sand and is sold as sandpit sand.

"We've just put a climbing frame and swing in the garden. How can we soften any falls?"

Cover the immediate area with an 8 cm (3 in) layer of bark chippings. You can also buy special play area flooring tiles.